At Home in the World

At Home in the World

Stories and Essential Teachings
from a Monk's Life

Thich Nhat Hanh

**PARALLAX
PRESS**

BERKELEY, CALIFORNIA

Parallax Press
P.O. Box 7355
Berkeley, California 94707
parallax.org

Parallax Press is the publishing division of Plum Village
Community of Engaged Buddhism, Inc.

Stories from this book are adapted from both unpublished talks
and previously published works by Thich Nhat Hanh.

The Thich Nhat Hanh Foundation supports Thich Nhat
Hanh's peace work and mindfulness teachings around the
world. For more information on how you can help, visit
www.thichnhathanhfoundation.org. Thank you.

Edited by Rachel Neumann and the
Plum Village Editorial Team.

Cover and text design by Debbie Berne
Illustrations © Jason DeAntonis
Cover photo © Karen Hagen Liste

Jason DeAntonis is an award-winning Bay Area artist known
for his fine carpentry, sculpture, painting, printmaking, and
book illustration.

ISBN: 978-1-946764-39-3

Library of Congress Cataloging-in-Publication Data for hardcover

Names: Nhat Hanh, Thich, author.
Title: At home in the world : stories and essential teachings
    from a monk's life / Thich Nhat Hanh.
Description: Berkeley, California : Parallax Press, 2016.
Identifiers: LCCN 2016051091 | ISBN 9781941529423
Subjects: LCSH: Nhat Hanh, Thich. | Buddhists—
    Biography. | Buddhism—Doctrines.
Classification: LCC BQ9800.T5392 N45765 2016 | DDC
    294.3/927092 [B]—dc23
LC record available at https://lccn.loc.gov/2016051091

Printed on 30% post-consumer waste recycled paper

1 2 3 4 / 22 21 20 19

Teaching is not done by talking alone.
It is done by how you live your life.
My life is my teaching. My life is my message.

THICH NHAT HANH

contents

At Home in the World 11

Life in Vietnam 15

Eating My Cookie 16

Time to Live 17

The Joy of Having Toilets 18

The Leaf 19

Drawing of the Buddha 20

Kaleidoscope 22

The Hermit and the Well 23

Gifts from My Teacher 26

My Master's Robe 28

Banana Leaves 31

Cherry Tree in Bloom 32

Closing the Door 34

Ria Greens 36

Washing Dishes 37

Durian 39

Voice of the Rising Tide 40

War and Exile 43

The Last Sack of Rice 44

A French Soldier 46

Fresh Herbs 53

Not Giving Up 54

The Use of Seeing 56

The Airfield 57

Heat 59

At Sea on Solid Ground 61

The Coconut Monk 67

Mindfulness in the Battle Zone 69

The Petition 71

Martin Luther King Jr., Bodhisattva 72

Prisoner of Conscience 74

I'm from the Center 75

This Is Not China 76

Alfred Hassler 77

Call Me By My True Names 79

Healing the Wounds of War 82

Practice Is a Boat 85

First Blossoms 87

The Bamboo Grove 88

The Blossoming of Plum Village 89

Hermitage in the Wind 90

Enjoy Your Sleeping Bag 92

The Peugeot 95

Mr. Mounet and the Cedar Trees 96

Umbrella Pines 100

Binding Books 103

Apple Juice and Pinecones 104

The Happiness of Writing 106

Lotus Tea 108

Brother and Sister 109

The Linden Tree 110

Learning to Hug 111

Nails 112

Tangerine Meditation 113

Raking Leaves 115

Breathing and Scything 117

The Mathematics Teacher 118

A Palm Tree in My Garden 120

I Am in Love 122

An Old Tree Produces New
   Blossoms *125*
Hide-and-Seek *126*

At Home in the World *129*
Greeting Each Other *130*
The Bell *131*
The Soul of Ancient Europe *133*
A Marketplace Dream *135*
Footsteps of the Buddha *138*
Two Minutes of Peace *140*
Drops of Compassion *142*
The Times of India *144*
A Relaxing Bus Ride *146*
Olive Trees *148*
Walking Freely *149*

I Have Arrived *151*
A Classroom Dream *152*
Lettuce *154*
Our Two Hands *155*
Look into Your Hand *156*
Give Me Some Tobacco! *158*
The Wave and the Water *161*
The Googleplex *162*
Is the Buddha in the Car? *164*
Walking on Country Paths *166*
One Step *167*
Belonging *169*
Fierce and Gentle Bodhisattva *171*
The Astronaut *173*
Autumn Leaf *175*

Finding Home *176*

Life Is Our True Home *178*

I Am Not in Here *180*

About Thich Nhat Hanh *183*

At Home in the World

In 1968 during the Vietnam War, I went to France to represent the
Vietnamese Buddhist Peace Delegation at the Paris Peace Talks.
Our mission was to speak out against the war on behalf of the mass
of Vietnamese people whose voices were not being heard. I was
flying back from Japan, where I had been to give a public talk, and
stopped in New York on the way to see my friend Alfred Hassler, of
the Fellowship of Reconciliation, an organization working actively to
end the Vietnam war and promote social justice. But I didn't have
a transit visa, so when I landed in Seattle I was taken aside and led
to a room where I was locked in and not permitted to see or speak
to anyone. The walls were covered with Wanted posters picturing
wanted felons. The authorities took my passport and wouldn't allow
me to contact anyone. It wasn't until several hours later, when my
flight was about to leave, that it was finally returned to me and I was
escorted to the plane.

Two years earlier, in 1966, I was in Washington, DC, for a conference when a Baltimore Sun reporter informed me of a dispatch
from Saigon urging the governments of the US, France, the United
Kingdom, and Japan to no longer honor my passport because they
felt I had been saying things opposing their efforts in the war against
Communism. The governments complied, and my passport was
invalidated. Some of my friends in Washington, DC, urged me to go
into hiding, but to stay in the US would have meant risking deporta-
tion and jail.

So I didn't go into hiding and instead sought political asylum in
France. The French government granted me asylum, and I was able
to obtain an *apatride* travel document. *Apatride* means you don't
belong to any country; you become stateless. With this document,

I could travel to any European country that had signed the Geneva Convention. But to go to countries like Canada or the US, I would still need to apply for a visa, which is very difficult to do when you are no longer a citizen of any country. My original intention had been to only leave Vietnam for three months in order to give a series of lectures at Cornell University, and to make a speaking tour of the US and Europe to call for peace, and then to go home again. My family, all my friends and coworkers—my whole life—was in Vietnam. Yet I ended up being exiled for almost forty years.

Whenever I applied for a visa to go to the US, it would be turned down automatically. The government didn't want me to go there; they believed I might harm the US war effort in Vietnam. I wasn't allowed to go to the US and I wasn't allowed to go to England either. I would have to write letters to such people as Senator George McGovern and Senator Robert Kennedy asking them to send me a letter of invitation. Their replies read something like this: "Dear Thich Nhat Hanh, I would like to know more about the situation of the war in Vietnam. Please come and inform me. If you have difficulties obtaining a visa, please telephone me at this number . . . " Only with such a letter could I get a visa. Otherwise, it was impossible.

I have to admit that the first two years of exile were quite difficult. Although I was already a forty-year-old monk with many disciples, I had still not yet found my true home. I could give very good lectures on the practice of Buddhism, but I had not truly arrived. Intellectually, I knew a lot about Buddhism: I had trained for many years in the Buddhist Institute and had been practicing since I was sixteen, but I hadn't yet really found my true home.

My intention on the speaking tours in the US was to bring people information about the real situation in Vietnam that they weren't hearing about on the radio and in the newspaper. During the tour, I would only sleep one or two nights in each city I visited. There were times when I woke up at night and didn't know where I was. It was very hard. I had to breathe in and out and remember what city and country I was in.

During this time, I had a recurring dream of being at home in my root temple in central Vietnam. I would be climbing a green hill covered with beautiful trees when, halfway to the top, I would wake up and realize that I was in exile. The dream came to me over and over again. In the meantime, I was very active, learning how to play with children from many countries: German children, French children, American children, and English children. I was making friends with Anglican priests, Catholic priests, Protestant ministers, rabbis, imams, and others. My practice was the practice of mindfulness. I tried to live in the here and now and touch the wonders of life every day. It was thanks to this practice that I survived. The trees in Europe were so different from the trees in Vietnam. The fruits, the flowers, the people, they were all completely different. The practice brought me back to my true home in the here and now. Eventually I stopped suffering, and the dream did not come back anymore.

People may think that I was suffering because I wasn't allowed to go back to my home in Vietnam. But that's not the case. When I was finally allowed to return, after almost forty years of exile, it was a joy to be able to offer the teachings and practices of mindfulness and Engaged Buddhism to the monks, nuns, and laypeople there; and it was a joy to have time to talk to artists, writers, and scholars. Nevertheless, when it was time to leave my native country again, I didn't suffer.

The expression, "I have arrived, I am home," is the embodiment of my practice. It is one of the main Dharma seals of Plum Village. It expresses my understanding of the teaching of the Buddha and is the essence of my practice. Since finding my true home, I no longer suffer. The past is no longer a prison for me. The future is not a prison either. I am able to live in the here and now and to touch my true home. I am able to arrive home with every breath and with every step. I don't have to buy a ticket; I don't have to go through a security check. Within a few seconds, I can arrive home.

When we are deeply in touch with the present moment, we can touch both the past and the future; and if we know how to handle the present moment properly, we can heal the past. It was precisely because I did not have a country of my own that I had the opportunity to find my true home. This is very important. It was because I didn't belong to any particular country that I had to make an effort to break through and find my true home. The feeling that we are not accepted, that we do not belong anywhere and have no national identity, can provoke the breakthrough necessary for us to find our true home.

Life in Vietnam

Eating My Cookie

When I was four years old, my mother used to bring me a cookie every time she returned from the market. I would go to the front yard and take my time eating it, sometimes taking half an hour or forty-five minutes to eat one cookie. I would take a small bite and look up at the sky. Then I would touch the dog with my feet and take another small bite. I just enjoyed being there, with the sky, the earth, the bamboo thickets, the cat, the dog, the flowers. I was able to spend so much time eating my cookie because I did not have much to worry about. I was not thinking about the future; I was not regretting the past. I was dwelling entirely in the present moment, with my cookie, the dog, the bamboo thickets, the cat, and everything.

It is possible to eat our meals as slowly and joyfully as I ate the cookie of my childhood. Maybe you have the impression that you have lost the cookie of your childhood, but I am sure it is still there, somewhere in your heart. Everything is still there, and if you really want it, you can find it. Eating mindfully is a most important practice of meditation. We can eat in a way that we can bring back to life the cookie of our childhood. The present moment is filled with joy and happiness. If you are attentive, you will see it.

Time to Live

Life in Vietnam when I was young was quite different from the way it is now. A birthday party, a poetry reading, or the anniversary of a family member's death would last all day, not only a few hours. You could arrive and leave at any time. You didn't need to have a car or a bike—you just walked. If you lived far away, you set out the day before and spent the night at a friend's house along the way. No matter what time you arrived, you were welcomed and served food. When the first four people had arrived, they were served together at a table. If you were the fifth, you waited until three others came so you could eat together with them.

The word "leisure" in Chinese is written with the character for door or window. Inside the door or window, there is the character for moon. It means that only when you are truly at leisure do you have time to see and enjoy the moon. Today, most of us don't have such luxury. We have more money and more material comfort, but we aren't really happier because we simply do not have time to enjoy each other's company.

There is a way to live our daily life that transforms normal life into a spiritual life. Even very simple things, like drinking tea with mindfulness can be a deeply spiritual experience, which can enrich our lives. Why would people spend two hours just drinking one cup of tea? From a business viewpoint, this is a waste of time. But time is not money. Time has much more value than money. Time is life. Money is nothing compared with life. In two hours of drinking tea together, we don't get money, but we do get life.

The Joy of Having Toilets

Some people may ask, "How can I possibly be happy cleaning the toilet?" But in fact we're lucky to have a toilet to clean. When I was a novice monk in Vietnam, we didn't have any toilets at all. I lived in a temple with over one hundred people and not a single toilet, and yet we managed to survive. Around the temple there were bushes and hills, so we just went up on the hill. There were no rolls of toilet paper up on the hill—you had to take dry banana leaves or hope to find some dead leaves you could use. Even when I was a child at home, before becoming a monk, we didn't have a toilet either. Only very few people were rich enough to have toilets. Everybody else had to go into the rice fields or up on the hill. At that time, there were twenty-five million people in Vietnam, most of them without toilets. So having a toilet to clean at all can be enough to make us happy. We can be truly happy when we recognize that we already have more than enough conditions for happiness.

The Leaf

One day when I was a child, I looked into the large clay water jar in the front yard that we used for collecting water and I saw a very beautiful leaf at the bottom. It had so many colors. I wanted to take it out and play with it, but my arm was too short to reach the bottom. So I used a stick to try to get it out. It was so difficult I became impatient. I stirred twenty times, thirty times, and yet the leaf didn't come up to the surface. So I gave up and threw the stick away.

When I came back a few minutes later, I was surprised to see the leaf floating on the surface of the water, and I picked it up. While I was away the water had continued to turn, and had brought the leaf up to the surface. This is how our unconscious mind works. When we have a problem to solve, or when we want more insight into a situation, we need to entrust the task of finding a solution to the deeper level of our consciousness. Struggling with our thinking mind will not help.

Before going to sleep you may say to yourself: "Tomorrow I want to wake up at 4:30." The next day you naturally wake up at 4:30. Our unconscious mind, which in Buddhism is called our "store consciousness," knows how to listen. It collaborates with the thinking part of our mind that we use a lot in daily life. When we meditate, we don't only use our mind consciousness; we need to use and trust our store consciousness. When we plant the seed of a question or problem in our consciousness, we need to trust that eventually an insight will rise to the surface. Deep breathing, looking deeply, and allowing ourselves simply to be, will help our store consciousness offer the best insight.

Drawing of the Buddha

When I was a small boy of seven or eight, I happened to see a drawing of the Buddha on the cover of a Buddhist magazine. The Buddha was sitting on the grass, very peacefully, and I was impressed. I thought the artist must have had a lot of peace and calm within himself at the time to be able to draw such a special image. Just looking at the drawing made me happy, because so many people around me at the time were not very calm or happy at all.

Seeing this peaceful image, the idea came to me that I wanted to become someone like that Buddha, someone who could sit very still and calm. I think that was the moment when I first wanted to become a monk, although I didn't know how to describe it that way at the time.

The Buddha is not a god; he was very much a human being like the rest of us. Like many of us, he suffered greatly as a teenager. He saw the suffering in his kingdom and he saw how his father, King Suddhodana, tried to reduce the suffering around him, but seemed to be helpless. To young Siddhartha, politics seemed ineffective. Even as a teenager, he was searching for a way out of suffering. Although he had been born a prince, all the material comforts were not enough to make him happy, at home, or at peace. He left the palace where he was raised in order to find a way out of suffering and to find his true home.

I think that many young people today feel the same as the young Siddhartha. We are searching for something good, true, and beautiful to follow. But looking around we can't find what we're looking for and we become disillusioned. Even when I was very young, I had that kind of feeling in me. That's why, when I saw the drawing of the Buddha, I was so happy. I just wanted to be like him.

I learned that if I practiced well, I could be like a buddha. Anyone who is peaceful, loving, and understanding can be called a buddha. There were many buddhas in the past, there are buddhas in the present moment, and there will be many buddhas in the future. Buddha is not the name of a particular person; buddha is just a common name to designate anyone who has a high degree of peace and who has a high degree of understanding and compassion. All of us are capable of being called by this name.

Kaleidoscope

When I was a child, I used to enjoy playing with a kaleidoscope that I made from a tube and a few pieces of ground glass. When I turned the tube, many wonderful patterns and colors revealed themselves. Every time I made a small movement of my fingers, one image would disappear and give way to the next. I didn't cry at all when the first spectacle disappeared, because I knew that nothing was lost; another beautiful sight always followed.

When we look into a kaleidoscope, we see a beautiful symmetrical image; and whenever we turn the kaleidoscope, the image disappears. Can we describe this as a birth or a death? Or is the image merely a manifestation? After this manifestation, there's another manifestation that's equally beautiful—nothing is lost. I have seen people die very peacefully, with a smile, because they understand that birth and death are only waves on the surface of the ocean, not the ocean itself, just like the beautiful images in the kaleidoscope.

There is no birth and no death. There is only continuation.

The Hermit and the Well

When I was growing up, I lived in the province of Thanh Hoa in North Vietnam. One day, our schoolteacher told us that we were going on a trip to the top of a nearby mountain called Na Son. He told us that on top of the mountain there lived a hermit—a monk who lived alone and sat quietly day and night to become calm and peaceful like the Buddha. I had never met a hermit before, and I was very excited.

The day before the trip, we prepared some food for our picnic. We cooked rice, rolled it into balls, and wrapped them in banana leaves. We prepared sesame seeds, peanuts, and salt to dip the rice in. We also boiled some water to bring along. Early the next morning, we set out for a long hike to reach the foot of the mountain. Once there, my friends and I started to climb as quickly as we could. We did not know how to practice walking meditation yet. We walked very fast all the way up the mountain.

When we reached the top, we were very tired. We had drunk all of our water on the way up. I looked around for the hermit but did not see him anywhere. I only saw his hut made of bamboo and straw. Inside I discovered a small cot and an altar made of bamboo, but no hermit. Maybe he had heard us coming up the mountain and was hiding somewhere away from the noise and the many children.

It was time to have lunch, but I wasn't hungry. I was so disappointed that I hadn't seen the hermit. I left my friends and started climbing further up the mountain hoping to find him. As I walked deeper into the forest, I heard the sound of dripping water. It was a beautiful sound. I started to climb in the direction of that sound, and soon I found a natural well, a small pool surrounded by big rocks of many colors. The water was so clear that I could see all the way to the bottom. I was very thirsty. I knelt down, scooped some water in my palms, and drank it. The water tasted so good. I had never tasted anything as good as that water. I felt completely satisfied; I did not need or want anything at all—even the desire to meet the hermit was gone. I had the feeling that I had met the hermit. I imagined that perhaps the hermit had transformed himself into the well.

I was tired. I lay down on the ground to rest so I could spend a few more minutes with the well. I looked up and saw the branch of a tree against the blue sky. I closed my eyes and soon I fell into a deep sleep. I don't know how long I slept. When I woke up, I didn't know where I was. Then I saw the branch of the tree against the sky and the wonderful well. I remembered everything.

It was time to go back to join my classmates. Reluctantly I said goodbye to the well and began to walk back down. As I walked out of the forest, from deep within me a sentence came to my mind. It was like a one-line poem: *I have tasted the most delicious water in the world.*

I sat down to eat with my friends. They were glad to see me and asked me where I had been, but I had no desire to talk. I wanted to cherish and keep my experience to myself a little longer, as it had touched me deeply. I sat down on the ground and ate my lunch quietly. The rice and the sesame seeds tasted so good.

It was many years ago that I climbed that mountain. But the image of the well and the quiet, peaceful sound of the dripping water are still alive inside me. You too may have met your hermit. Maybe as a rock, a tree, a star, or a beautiful sunset.

That was my first spiritual experience. After that I became calmer and quieter. I didn't feel the need to share what had happened. I wanted to keep it in my heart. My intention to become a monk became stronger. At the age of sixteen I received my parents' permission to enter Tu Hieu Temple near Hue and practice as an aspirant and then as a novice.

Gifts from My Teacher

When I became a novice monk at the age of sixteen, I received a gift from my teacher. It was a book of fifty practice poems called "Gathas for Everyday Use" compiled by a great Chinese Zen master. Using gathas to help us become aware of our everyday actions is a Zen monastic tradition going back over a thousand years.

So the very first book I received to learn from was a book of poetry. Strange! As novices we had to memorize all these poems in order to practice. In my tradition, poetry has a lot to do with meditation, as do music and art. The verses in the book were four-line poems in classical Chinese, and every line had only five words, so each poem had twenty words in all. One poem was for sitting down. You sit down in such a way that you generate the energy of mindfulness. There was even a poem for putting on your undershirt or your monk's robe. Every daily activity can be done in poetry and in mindfulness. I like that practice very much.

There was also a poem to recite when lighting a lamp. In my time, there was no electricity in the temple, and no running water. So we used kerosene lamps; and when you lit the lamp, you would recite the poem silently. There was another for lighting a candle. I was very happy as a young novice monk. We had a lot of time to practice, and we also had time to play outside and enjoy ourselves.

Later, as a fully-ordained monk, I thought that the poems should be translated into modern Vietnamese, so they would be more natural to practice with. So I translated them all into Vietnamese. Now they exist in English, French, German, and many other languages and are available for every one of us to enjoy and practice with.

Elements of monastic culture can also be experienced by people who live in society. When I met the Trappist monk Thomas Merton in his monastery in Kentucky in 1966, we enjoyed discussing this. Walking meditation, using gathas, and practicing mindful breathing can easily be applied to daily life. For many years I have been sharing monastic culture with lay friends and fellow practitioners. There are many friends everywhere in the world who practice brushing their teeth with the poem for tooth brushing, or who practice putting on their overcoat with the poem for putting on a coat.

In my time there were bicycles, but the monks didn't ride them. In the old days monks rode horses, but not bicycles. I was one of the first Buddhist monks in Vietnam to ride a bicycle. At that time it was not considered a very "monkish" thing to do. One day, six of us young monks decided to try, so we rented six bicycles and we learned how to ride. Then we continued to use bicycles. At the time, people were surprised. Now monks drive cars, and it's even quicker. But at that time, to see a monk on a bicycle was very new. Since we rode with joy and awareness, we were practicing bicycle meditation. I even wrote a poem for riding a bicycle, and later on I wrote a poem for driving a car as well. Poems like these can help us live each moment deeply, in awareness and in touch with the spiritual dimension of life.

My Master's Robe

My monastic ordination at Tu Hieu Temple was scheduled for four o'clock in the morning. The night before, after chanting practice, I saw my teacher sitting in his room on a cushion beside the light of a flickering candle; there was a stack of old scriptures piled high on a table next to him. He was carefully mending a tear in an old brown robe. Despite his old age, he still had clear vision and a straight posture. Brother Tam Man and I stopped at the entrance and watched. As he slowly pulled the needle through the cloth, my teacher looked like a *bodhisattva* in deep meditation.

After a moment, we entered the room and my teacher looked up. Seeing us, he nodded and then lowered his head to continue sewing a half-sewn stitch. Brother Tam Man spoke: "Respected teacher, please go and rest; it is already very late."

My teacher did not look up. "Let me finish sewing this robe so that Quan can wear it tomorrow morning."

Then I understood why my teacher had been sorting through his pile of old robes all afternoon; he was looking for the least worn robe to fix and make presentable for me. Tomorrow for the first time I would wear a brown robe. During the past three years as aspirants, we were only allowed to wear the gray robe. Once ordained as a novice, I would be allowed to put on the precious robe that the *sutras* call the robe of liberation, the uniform of freedom.

In a wavering voice I said, "Respected teacher, let us ask Auntie Tu to finish the sewing."

"No, I want to sew it for you with my own hands," he replied softly.

There was silence.

With our arms folded in an obedient manner, we stood to one side not daring to say another word. A little later, without raising his eyes from the needle, my teacher spoke.

"Have you heard the story in the sutra about a great disciple during the time of the Buddha who attained enlightenment just from sewing robes?

"Let me tell it to you," he continued. "This disciple often found joy and peace in mending torn robes; he mended his own and also those of his Dharma brothers. Each time he passed the needle through the fabric, he gave rise to a wholesome goodness that had the power to liberate. One day, when the needle was passing through the fabric, he gained insight about a most deep and wonderful teaching, and in six consecutive stitches he attained the six miraculous powers."

I turned my head and looked at my teacher with deep affection and respect. My teacher might not have attained the six miraculous powers, but he had reached a profound stage of understanding and insight.

At last the robe was mended. My teacher signaled for me to come closer. He asked me to try it on. The robe was a little too large for me, but that did not prevent me from feeling so happy that I was moved to tears. I had received the most sacred kind of love—a pure love that was gentle and spacious, which nourished and infused my aspiration through my many years of training and practice.

My teacher handed me the robe. I received it knowing it was tremendous encouragement and that it was given with a tender and discreet love. My teacher's voice at that moment was probably the gentlest and sweetest I had ever heard:

"I mended this myself so that tomorrow you will have it to wear, my child."

It was so simple. But I was deeply moved when I heard these words. Although it wasn't yet time for the ordination ceremony and I was not yet kneeling before the Buddha, uttering the great vow to save all beings, my heart made the vast and deep vow with all sincerity to live a life of service. Brother Tam Man looked at me with wholehearted affection and respect. In that moment, the universe for us was truly a universe of fragrant flowers.

Since that day, I have had many new robes. The new brown robes are given attention for some time but later on they are forgotten. But the old torn brown robe from my past will always remain holy. Today, the robe is too torn to be worn, but I still hold on to it so that in moments of reflection I can look back on the beautiful memories of the past.

Banana Leaves

When I was a young monk in Vietnam, I realized something while meditating on a young banana plant, which had three leaves. The first leaf had completely unfurled and was exposed to the sun and rain and was enjoying her new life as a leaf. The second leaf was still unfurling, not yet fully open. The third leaf, the younger sister, was not yet open.

I noticed that as the first leaf unfolded, she was also helping her younger sisters to grow. She unfolded and enjoyed the sunshine and the rain. She sang every time the wind blew. The first and second leaves saw themselves in the third leaf. When the time came for the first leaf to wither and dry up, she did not cry. She knew that she would live on in the second and third leaves. Eventually, she went back to the soil and served as nourishment for the whole banana tree and the other leaves that came after her.

Our lives have meaning like this. We are here to do something. We have a purpose. Looking deeply into the first leaf, I could see myself. By enjoying my life, I was nourishing my younger sisters and brothers and transmitting joy, hope, and the best of myself to them. They, in turn, helped me to nourish our other siblings not yet born. Thanks to the wisdom of nondiscrimination, called *upeksha* in Sanskrit, we do not fight, quarrel, or compete with one another. When we are not caught in the notion of being a separate self from other human beings, there can be harmony between us. When I teach a friend how to practice meditation, I don't call myself "teacher," and my friend "student." There is no transmitter and no receiver. We are one and the same. Together, we help each other grow.

Cherry Tree in Bloom

In the old times in Vietnam, when your cherry tree was about to bloom, you would take the opportunity to organize a reception to celebrate the occasion. You would predict on which day the blossoms would be perfect, and you would spend time writing personal cards inviting friends to come. You would prepare everything to ensure your friends would be able to enjoy a wonderful tea with you, and there would be a special delicacy, perhaps even wheat-germ cookies, to have with the tea.

In Vietnam we used to pick the best kind of wheat when it was still young and put it in warm water to sprout. Once it sprouted, we would cook it and condense it into a kind of paste. We didn't put sugar in it, yet it was still a little bit sweet from the fermentation. We concentrated it until it was very thick. Then we would go to the river and pick up small pebbles, wash them very thoroughly, and dry them in the sunshine. We would cover the pebbles with the wheat-germ paste and dry them again, so that each pebble was caked in wheat-germ paste. That is what our ancestors used to eat when they drank their tea. It took a lot of love and energy to prepare that kind of "cookie"—you might call it a cookie, but it wasn't really a cookie, because if you were to bite into it the way you bite into a cookie, you would break your teeth.

On the day of your special event, you would clean the house thoroughly, and there would be the tree in bloom, the pebble cookies, and tea. Sometimes the weather might suddenly become cooler, and the cherry blossoms wouldn't have enough time to bloom before the event. In that case, people would bring a drum to the foot of the cherry tree, and play the drum to stimulate the flowers to bloom.

That's the way it was in the past. It may sound childish, but it was very poetic and very beautiful.

When everyone arrived, we would welcome them in the garden. The atmosphere was very festive: your friends were coming to your home; it was a big event. All the children and grandchildren would come out to celebrate and experience this kind of sacred celebration, and the joyful atmosphere of relaxation, freedom, and friendship. People didn't have to teach their children or grandchildren how to stop and celebrate; the children just experienced it and joined in by themselves.

You may not have such an elaborate ritual to celebrate trees in bloom with your friends, and you probably don't have wheat-germ paste pebble cookies. But still, taking time to create a special moment to drink tea or eat a meal together with joy, beauty, and simplicity can initiate your children into a spiritual life.

Closing the Door

Children sometimes ask me, "Why do you meditate?" I meditate because I love it. But I don't just love sitting meditation, I also love meditating while walking or even while standing. Suppose you need to stand in line, waiting for your turn to buy or serve yourself some food. You can take the opportunity to practice mindful breathing, aware of your in-breath and your out-breath, enjoying yourself and the presence of the people around you.

Meditation can be very informal. When you drive, if you drive with mindfulness, enjoying your in-breath and out-breath, we can say you are practicing meditation. When you wash the dishes, if you enjoy breathing in and breathing out and you smile, the dishwashing becomes very pleasant. I enjoy washing dishes very much. Washing dishes is not only to have clean dishes, but to simply enjoy the time of washing dishes. With the energy of mindfulness, every action in our daily life can become pleasurable.

I practice this lesson every day. One day, when I was a novice monk, my teacher asked me to do something for him. I was very excited to do it for him, because I loved my teacher very much. So I rushed out to do it. But because I was so excited, I wasn't mindful enough, and I slammed the door on my way out. My teacher called me back and said: "My child. Please go out and close the door again. But this time, do better than you did before." Hearing his words, I knew that my practice had been lacking. So I bowed to my teacher and walked to the door with all of my being, every step with mindfulness. I went out and, very mindfully, closed the door after me. My teacher did not have to tell me a second time. Now every time I open and close a door, I do so with mindfulness, remembering my teacher.

Many years later, I was in Kentucky with Thomas Merton, the

Trappist monk, and I told him that story. He said: "Well, I noticed that without you telling me; I have seen the way you close the door." A month after I left his monastery in Kentucky, he gave a talk to his students and told them the story of me closing the door.

One day many years later, a Catholic woman from Germany came on retreat to our Plum Village practice center in France. On her last day, she told us that she had come only out of curiosity. She had listened to a recording of Thomas Merton's talk, and she had come to see how I closed the door.

Ria Greens

The montagnards, the indigenous people who lived near our hermitage in the mountainous forests of the Central Highlands of Vietnam, sold many things they harvested from the forest to city-dwellers—bamboo, rattan, orchids, and venison—but they never sold *ria* greens. They told us that these greens prevented leg cramps. I think they also contain elements that relieve arthritis, and Uncle Dai Ha used to say that they were a good cure for insomnia. From time to time, we would pick some precious ria greens and ask Aunt Tam Hue to make soup from them. But our montagnard friends did not prepare soup from the greens. Instead they would crush the leaves, add a little salt, and then steam them. It was their favorite dish. One afternoon, Miss Phuong, who was a botany professor, came from Saigon. She gathered some greens that she thought were ria greens and made soup. After consuming the "ria" soup, we all felt a little high. We had a lot of fun teasing our good-natured friend about that—the botanist who couldn't recognize the right greens!

Washing Dishes

When I was still a novice at Tu Hieu Pagoda, washing the dishes was hardly a pleasant task. During the annual Rains' retreat, all the monks would come back to the monastery to practice together for three months, and sometimes we were only two novices who had to do all the cooking and wash all the dishes for well over a hundred monks. There was no soap. We had only ashes, rice husks, and coconut husks, and that was all. Cleaning such a high stack of bowls was a difficult chore, especially during the winter when the water was freezing cold. Then we had to heat up a big pot of water before we could do any scrubbing. Nowadays with liquid soap, special scrub pads, and even hot running water, it is much easier to enjoy washing the dishes.

To my mind, the idea that doing dishes is unpleasant can occur only when you aren't doing them. Once you are standing in front of the sink with your sleeves rolled up and your hands in the warm water, it is really quite pleasant. I enjoy taking my time with each dish, being fully aware of the dish, the water, and each movement of my hands. I know that if I hurry in order to be able to finish so I can sit down sooner and eat dessert or enjoy a cup of tea, the time of washing dishes will be unpleasant and not worth living. That would be a pity, for each minute, each second of life is a miracle. The dishes themselves and the fact that I am here washing them are miracles!

If I am incapable of washing dishes joyfully, if I want to finish them quickly so I can go and have dessert or a cup of tea, I will be equally incapable of enjoying my dessert or my tea when I finally have them. With the fork in my hand, I will be thinking about what to do next, and the texture and the flavor of the dessert, together with the pleasure of eating it, will be lost. I will be constantly dragged into the future, miss out on life altogether, and never able to live in the present moment.

Each thought, each action in the sunlight of awareness becomes sacred. In this light, no boundary exists between the sacred and the profane. I must confess it takes me a bit longer to do the dishes, but I live fully in every moment, and I am happy. Washing the dishes is at the same time a means and an end. We do the dishes not only in order to have clean dishes, we also do the dishes just to do the dishes, to live fully in each moment while washing them, and to be truly in touch with life.

Durian

In Southeast Asia, many people are extremely fond of a large, thorny fruit called durian, whose smell is extremely strong. You might even say that some are addicted to it. There are those who, when they finish eating the fruit, put the skin under their bed so they can continue to enjoy the smell of it. To me, the smell of durian is horrendous.

One day when I was practicing chanting alone in my temple in Vietnam, it happened that there was a durian on the altar which had been offered to the Buddha. I was trying to recite the Lotus Sutra, using a wooden drum and a large bowl-shaped bell for accompaniment, but I could not concentrate at all, because of the smell. I finally decided to turn the bell over and imprison the durian so I could continue to chant the sutra. After I finished, I bowed to the Buddha and liberated the durian.

If you were to say to me, "I love you so much I would like you to eat some of this durian," I would suffer terribly. You may say you love me, and that you want me to be happy, but yet you want me to eat durian. That is an example of love without understanding. Your intention is good, but you don't have the correct understanding.

When you love someone, you want the other person to be happy. If they are not happy, there is no way you can be happy. Happiness is not an individual matter. True love requires deep understanding. In fact, love is another name for understanding. If you do not understand, you cannot love properly. Without understanding, your love will only cause the other person to suffer.

Voice of the Rising Tide

When I was a young monk at the Buddhist Institute in Saigon, I was something of a revolutionary monk. I wanted Buddhism to be able to help liberate and unite the Vietnamese people, but the teachings did not give any specific ways for us to practice so that we could do this. A group of us felt that unless we renewed Buddhist teachings and practices, they would be unable to offer appropriate concrete practices that could unite us and help abolish social injustice and war.

The first step we undertook was to publish a newsletter to express our ideas. At that time we did not have photocopy machines; we didn't have even a mimeograph machine. Each student monk would write an article, and then we would bind them together to make a newsletter. We were very ambitious and titled the magazine the *Voice of the Rising Tide*. The sound of the rising tide is the sound that transcends all worldly sounds. The magazine was passed from hand-to-hand and everybody in the Buddhist Institute read it. Some of our teachers loved it because the ideas it expressed were new, refreshing, and stimulating, but other teachers felt we were dangerous, and they banned the magazine.

Many of our teachers at the Institute spoke about peace, compassion, nonself, and the happiness of living beings, but few of them did anything. They spoke of helping society, yet they took no concrete action to help the poor and oppressed. At that time, many young people in Vietnam were inspired to join political and revolutionary groups like the Communist Party and the Kuomintang. Dozens of political movements had mobilized to fight the French and force them out of the country, and many were struggling for social justice. When you are young, you want to do something for your country. Many young monastics were attracted to Marxist ideology and were tempted out of the monasteries to join these movements. They felt that Buddhist practice was outdated and was not responding to the real needs of the people.

Taking action against injustice is not enough. We believed action must embody mindfulness. If there is no awareness, action will only cause more harm. Our group believed it must be possible to combine meditation and action to create mindful action.

The Institute was so conservative and resistant to change that four of us decided to leave. We left behind a letter demanding the reformation and renewal of the way of teaching and practicing Buddhism. Our leaving was like a bell of mindfulness to say that if they didn't pay attention, then many other people at the Institute might leave. We wanted to set up a new community where we could study, teach, and practice Buddhism the way we thought it should be.

The Institute reacted very strongly. We were just four young monks and the Institute was very powerful. They knew we wanted to start something new, and they also knew that, because we were monks, we would have to seek refuge in another temple. Therefore, three days after we left, the Institute sent a letter to all the temples asking them not to harbor us.

It was a very difficult time. We did not have any money, but we had a monastic sister who lived in the south, so we took refuge in her home. After more friends came to support us, we were able to find land and build a small temple in the countryside where we could begin our practice. We had a lot of energy, motivation, and goodwill. We were not looking for money, power, or fame; we were looking for the kind of Buddhism that could help us change society and respond to the challenges of our times.

Five years after we moved to our new home, I went back to the Institute in Saigon. By then we had established a practicing community. I had also published a number of books and magazines on the application and renewal of Buddhism in the fields of economics, education, politics, and humanitarian action. By then the Institute had realized it needed to change if it didn't want to lose more people. It began to offer courses in philosophy, comparative religion, and science.

Several years later, in 1964, the Saigon Buddhist administration asked me to become editor-in-chief of a new weekly edition of the *Voice of the Rising Tide*, and I accepted. This time, a decade after our first hand-bound editions of the magazine, the *Voice of the Rising Tide* was properly printed, bound, and widely distributed. Our editorial team began reporting on the Buddhist community's work to help bring peace and reunify the country. Buddhists were speaking out, leading huge street protests and hunger strikes, and writing articles and letters. We also included whole sections of poetry from some of the most eloquent and radical poets of the time. The magazine soon became the most popular Buddhist weekly in Vietnam. Fifty thousand copies were printed every week, and they had to be flown by plane to Hue and Danang to meet demand.

While we were all working on the magazine in Saigon, I was living in a little thatched hermitage on the grounds of the Bamboo Forest Monastery, about an hour's motorbike ride from the city center. The monastic brothers living there helped make the monastery into a wonderful, happy place for us all to take refuge in. Every week we would come together to practice sitting meditation, walking meditation, and imagining a brighter future together. We were able to manifest what we had dreamed of: action that was rooted in practice that responded to people's needs. This experience showed us that engaged practice was not only possible, it was necessary if we were going to make real and peaceful change.

War and Exile

The Last Sack of Rice

In 1946 during the French-Indochina War, I was a novice monk at the Tu Hieu Temple in Hue, Central Vietnam. At that time, the city of Hue was occupied by the French army. One day two French soldiers arrived at our temple. While one stayed in the jeep outside the temple gate, the other came in, carrying a gun, and demanded all of our rice. We had only one sack of rice for all the monks and he wanted to take it away. The soldier was young, not yet twenty, and hungry. He looked thin and pale, as if he had malaria, which I also had at that time.

I had to obey his order to carry our heavy bag of rice to the jeep. It was a long distance, and as I staggered under the bag's precious weight, anger and unhappiness rose up in me. They were taking what little rice we had, leaving our community without any food. As I walked back into the temple, I was crying. Only later did I learn that one of the elder monks had secretly buried a large container of rice on the temple grounds, deep in the earth.

Many times over the years, I have meditated on this French soldier. I have seen that, still in his teens, he had to leave his parents, brothers, sisters, and friends to travel across the world to Vietnam, where he was faced with the horrors of killing my countrymen or being killed himself. I have often wondered whether this soldier survived the war and was able to return home to his parents. It is very likely that he did not survive. The French-Indochina War lasted many years, ending only with the French defeat at Dien Bien Phu and the Geneva Accords in 1954. After looking deeply, I came to realize that the Vietnamese were not the only victims of the war; the French soldiers were victims as well. With this insight, I no longer had any anger toward the young soldier. Instead compassion for him arose within me, and I only wished him well.

I did not know the French soldier's name and he did not know mine, but when we met we were already enemies. He came and was prepared to kill me for our food, and I had to comply in order to protect myself and my fellow monks. And yet the two of us were not, by nature, enemies. Under different circumstances, we could have become close friends, maybe even loving each other as brothers. It was the war that separated us and brought violence between us.

This is the nature of war: it turns us into enemies. People who have never met kill each other out of fear. War creates so much suffering—children become orphans, entire cities and villages are destroyed. All who suffer in such conflicts are victims. Coming from a background of such enormous devastation and suffering, and having experienced the French-Indochina and Vietnam Wars, I have a deep aspiration to prevent war from ever happening again.

It is my prayer that nations will no longer send their young people to fight each other, not even in the name of peace. I do not accept the concept of war for peace, nor of a "just war," in the same way that I cannot accept the concepts of "just slavery," "just hatred," or "just racism." During the wars in Vietnam, my friends and I declared ourselves neutral; we took no sides and we had no enemies, North or South, French, American, or Vietnamese.

A French Soldier

In 1947 I was in Hue, living and studying at the Buddhist Institute at
Bao Quoc Temple, not too far from my root temple where I had been
ordained into monastic life and where I normally lived. It was during
the First Indochina War. At that time, the French army was occupy-
ing the whole region and had set up a military base in Hue. We often
heard gunfire around us between French and Vietnamese soldiers.
People living high in the hills had set up small fortresses for protection. There were nights when the villagers shut themselves in their
homes, bracing themselves against the barrage. In the morning when
they awoke, they found corpses from the battle of the previous night,
and slogans written in whitewash mixed with blood on the road.
Occasionally monks would travel the remote paths in this region, but
hardly anyone else dared pass through the area—especially the city
dwellers of Hue, who had only recently returned after having been
evacuated. Even though Bao Quoc was situated near a train station,
hardly anyone risked going there, which speaks for itself!

One morning I set out from Bao Quoc for my monthly visit back
to my root temple. It was quite early; the dew was still on the tips of
the grass. Inside a cloth bag I carried my ceremonial robe and a few
sutras. In my hand, I carried the traditional Vietnamese cone-shaped
straw hat. I felt light and joyful at the thought of seeing my teacher,
my monastic brothers, and the ancient, highly venerated temple.

I had just gone over a hill, when I heard a voice call out. Up on
the hill, above the road, I saw a French soldier waving. Thinking he
was making fun of me because I was a monk, I turned away and
continued walking down the road. But suddenly I had the feeling that
this was no laughing matter. Behind me I heard the clomping of a
soldier's boots running up behind me. Perhaps he wanted to search

me; the cloth bag I was carrying could have looked suspicious to him. I stopped walking and waited. A young soldier with a thin, handsome face approached.

"Where are you going?" he asked in Vietnamese. From his pronunciation, I could tell that he was French and that his knowledge of Vietnamese was very limited.

I smiled and asked him in French, "If I were to reply in Vietnamese, would you understand?"

When he heard that I could speak French, his face lit up. He said he had no intention of searching me, and that he only wanted to ask me something. "I want to know which temple you're from," he said.

When I told him I was living at Bao Quoc Temple, he seemed interested.

"Bao Quoc Temple," he repeated. "Is that the big temple on the hill near the train station?"

When I nodded, he pointed up to a pump house on the side of the hill—his guard post apparently—and said, "If you're not too busy, please come up there with me so we can talk for a little while." We sat down near the pump house, and he told me about the visit he and five other soldiers had made ten days earlier to Bao Quoc Temple. They had gone to the temple at ten that night, in search of Vietnamese resistors, Viet Minh, who were reportedly gathering there.

"We were determined to find them. We carried guns. The orders were to arrest and even kill if necessary. But when we entered the temple we were stunned."

"Because there were so many Viet Minh?"

"No! No!" he exclaimed. "We wouldn't have been stunned if we had seen Viet Minh. We would have attacked no matter how many there were."

I was confused. "What surprised you?"

"What happened was so unexpected. Whenever we did searches in the past, people would run away or be thrown into a state of panic."

"People have been terrorized so many times that they run away in fear," I explained.

"I myself don't make a habit of terrorizing or threatening people," he replied. "Perhaps they are so frightened because they have been harmed by those who came before us.

"But when we entered the Bao Quoc Temple grounds, it was like entering a completely deserted place. The oil lamps were turned very low. We deliberately stomped our feet loudly on the gravel, and I had the feeling there were many people in the temple, but we couldn't hear anyone. It was incredibly quiet. The shouting of a comrade made me uneasy. No one replied. I turned on my flashlight and aimed it into the room we thought was empty—and I saw fifty or sixty monks sitting still and silent in meditation."

"That's because you came during our evening sitting period," I said, nodding my head.

"Yes. It was as if we'd run into a strange and invisible force," he said. "We were so taken aback that we turned and went back out to the courtyard. The monks just ignored us! They didn't raise a voice in reply, and they didn't show any sign of panic or fear."

"They weren't ignoring you; they were practicing concentrating on their breath—that was all."

"I felt drawn to their calmness," he admitted. "It really commanded my respect. We stood quietly in the courtyard at the foot of a large tree and waited for perhaps half an hour. Then a series of bells sounded, and the temple returned to normal activity. A monk lit a torch and came to invite us inside, but we simply told him why we were there and then took our leave. That day, I began to change my ideas about the Vietnamese people.

"There are many young men among us," he continued. "We are homesick; we miss our families and our country. We have been sent here to kill the Viet Minh, but we don't know if we will kill them or be killed by them and never return home to our families. Seeing the people here work so hard to rebuild their shattered lives reminds me of the shattered lives of my relatives in France after the Second World War. The peaceful and serene life of those monks makes me think about the lives of all human beings on Earth. And I wonder why we've come to this place. Why is the hatred between the Viet Minh and us so strong that we have traveled all the way over here to fight them?"

Deeply moved, I took his hand. I told him the story of an old friend of mine who had enlisted to fight the French, and who had been successful in winning many battles. One day my friend came to the temple where I was, and burst into tears as he embraced me. He told me that during an attack on a fortress, while he was concealed behind some rocks, he saw two young French soldiers sitting and talking. "When I saw the bright, handsome, innocent faces of those boys," he said, "I couldn't bear to open fire, dear Brother. People can label me weak and soft; they can say that if all the Vietnamese fighters were like me, it wouldn't be long before our whole country was overtaken. But for a moment I loved the enemy like my own mother loves me! I knew that the death of these two youngsters would make their mothers in France suffer, just as my mother had grieved for the death of my younger brother."

"So you see," I said to the French soldier, "that young Vietnamese soldier's heart was filled with the love of humanity."

The young French soldier sat quietly, lost in thought. Perhaps, like me, he was becoming more aware of the absurdity of the killing, the calamity of war, and the suffering of so many young people dying in an unjust and heartbreaking way.

The sun had already risen high in the sky, and it was time for me to go. The soldier told me that his name was Daniel Marty and he was twenty-one years old. He had just finished high school before coming to Vietnam. He showed me photographs of his mother and of a younger brother and sister. We parted with a feeling of understanding and friendship between us, and he promised to visit me at the temple on Sundays.

In the months that followed, he did visit me when he could, and I took him to our meditation hall to practice with me. I gave him the spiritual name Thanh Luong, meaning "pure and refreshing peaceful life." I taught him Vietnamese—he knew only the few phrases that he'd been taught by the military—and after a few months we were able to converse a little in my native tongue. He told me that he no longer had to go on raids as he had previously done, and I shared his relief. If there were letters from home, he showed them to me. Whenever he saw me, he joined his palms in greeting.

One day we invited Thanh Luong to a vegetarian meal at the temple. He accepted the invitation happily, and highly praised the delicious black olives and the flavorful dishes we served him. He found the fragrant mushroom rice soup my brother had prepared so delicious, he couldn't believe it was vegetarian. I had to explain to him in detail how it was made before he would believe it.

There were days when, sitting beside the temple tower, we would delve into conversations on spirituality and literature. When I praised French literature, Thanh Luong's eyes lit up with pride in his nation's culture. Our friendship became very deep.

Then one day when he came to visit, Thanh Luong announced that his unit would be moving to another area, and it was likely that he would soon be able to return to France. I walked him to the gate under the arch of the three portals of the temple and we hugged goodbye. "I will write you, Brother," he said.

"I will be very happy to receive your letter, and to reply."

A month later, I received a letter from him with the news that he would indeed return to France, but then go on to Algeria. He promised to write to me from there. I have not heard from him since. Who knows where Thanh Luong is now. Is he safe? But I know that when I last saw him, he was at peace. That moment of profound silence in the temple had changed him. He allowed the lives of all living beings to fill his heart, and he saw the senselessness and destructiveness of war. What made it all possible was that moment of complete and total stopping and opening to the powerful, healing, miraculous ocean called silence.

Fresh Herbs

During the Vietnam War, there were so many things to worry about. Bombs were falling every day and people were dying. My mind was completely focused on how to help stop the war, the killing, and the suffering. I thought I didn't have time to get in touch with the refreshing and healing wonders of life. Because of this belief, I didn't get the nourishment and nutrition that I so needed.

One day a young woman came to assist me in our work. She prepared a basket of fragrant Vietnamese herbs, the various kinds of fresh greens that we eat with every meal in Vietnam. I marveled at their beauty and aroma. I took a deep breath. Simply savoring that plate of fresh herbs was enough to restore my balance.

I had thought that I didn't have time to notice things like fragrant herbs, but in that moment I realized that I couldn't allow myself to be so completely immersed in the work. I also needed to take the time to live, to get in touch with the refreshing and healing elements inside me and around me.

As activists, we have a deep desire to succeed in our attempt to help the world. But if we don't maintain a balance between our work and the nourishment we need, we won't be very successful. The practice of walking meditation, mindful breathing, allowing our body and mind to rest, and getting in touch with the refreshing and healing elements inside and around us is crucial for our survival.

Not Giving Up

In 1964, the same year we started the new version of the *Voice
of the Rising Tide*, we established the School of Youth for Social
Service (SYSS). The SYSS trained thousands of young people to
go out to war-stricken remote villages to bring humanitarian relief.
One day we heard the news that Tra Loc, a village we had helped
build in Quang Tri Province, was bombed. It was very close to the
Demilitarized Zone (DMZ) separating the north and the south.
We—myself and fellow social workers of the SYSS—had spent more
than a year making the village into a beautiful place where people
could enjoy living. Then one day American planes came and bombed
the village. They had received information that Communist guerrillas
had infiltrated it.

The villagers lost their homes, and our social workers were
forced to take refuge elsewhere. They sent word to us and asked
whether they should rebuild the village. We said, "Yes, you have to
rebuild the village." We spent another six months rebuilding, and
then the village was destroyed a second time by bombing. Again,
the people lost their homes. We had built many villages across
the country, but it was very difficult near the DMZ. So our social
workers asked us whether we should rebuild it for a third time, and
after much deliberation we said, "Yes, we have to rebuild it." So we
rebuilt it for the third time. Do you know what happened? It was
destroyed for a third time by American bombing. We were very close
to despair.

Despair is the worst thing that can happen to a human being. We
had rebuilt the village a third time, and it had been bombarded for the
third time. Again the question was asked, "Should we rebuild? Should
we give up?" There was a lot of discussion at our headquarters, and

we were tempted by the idea of giving up—three times was too much. But in the end, we were wise enough not to give up. We saw that we could not afford *not* to rebuild. If we gave up on Tra Loc village, we would be giving up on hope. If we gave up hope, we would be overwhelmed by despair. And so we rebuilt the village a fourth time.

We desperately wanted to end the war, but we couldn't, because the situation was not in our hands—it was in the hands of big powers. It did not seem that there was any hope of an end, because the war had been dragging on for so long. I had to practice a lot of mindful breathing and coming back to myself. I have to confess I did not have a lot of hope at this time, but if I'd had *no* hope, it would have been devastating for these young people. I had to practice deeply and nourish the little hope I had inside so I could be a refuge for them. In difficult situations like these we have to go home and restore ourselves, to reestablish our solidity, freedom, peace, and calm so we can go on. This is why it is so important to have a spiritual dimension in our life.

I remember that about this time a group of young people came and sat with me and asked, "Dear Thay, do you have any hope that the war will end soon?" At that point, I could not see any sign of the war ending. But I did not want either them or myself to drown in an ocean of despair. I stayed silent for some time. Finally I said, "Dear friends, the Buddha said that everything is impermanent. The war has to end one day." The question is, what can we do to accelerate the impermanence? There *are* things we can do. It is very important to come home to ourselves and look deeply to see what we can do every day to help the situation. Taking action helps us not to drown in despair.

The Use of Seeing

During the Vietnam War, so many of our villages were bombed. My monastic brothers and sisters and I had to decide what to do. Should we continue to practice in our monasteries, or should we leave the meditation halls in order to offer spiritual and practical help to the people who were suffering under the bombs? After careful reflection, we decided to do both—to go out and help people and to do so in mindfulness. We called it Engaged Buddhism. Mindfulness must be *engaged*. Once we see that something needs to be done, we must take action. Seeing and acting go together. Otherwise, what is the use of seeing?

We must be aware of the real problems of the world. Then, with mindfulness, concentration, and insight, we will know what to do and what not to do in order to help. If we maintain awareness of our breathing and continue to practice equanimity, even in difficult situations, many people, animals, and plants will benefit from our way of doing things. Are you planting seeds of joy and peace? I try to do exactly that with every step. Peace is every step. Shall we continue our journey?

The Airfield

One day in 1964, I was sitting on a vacant airfield in the Central Highlands of Vietnam. It was during the war and I was waiting for a plane to go to Da Nang in the north, so I could assess the situation of the flooding there and help bring relief to the flood victims. The situation was very urgent, and so I had taken the first plane available—a military plane transporting blankets and clothing. However, this plane only went as far as Plei Ku in the Central Highlands. So I was sitting on the tarmac, alone, waiting for the next plane.

After some time, an American officer came by; he was also waiting for his plane. There were only the two of us at the airfield. I saw that he was a young US officer, and I had a lot of compassion for him. Why should he have to come to Vietnam to kill or to be killed? Out of compassion I said, "You must be very afraid of the Vietcong." The Vietcong were the Vietnamese Communist guerrillas. He immediately put his hand on his gun and asked me: "Are you a Vietcong?"

I realized then that my comment wasn't skillful; I had watered the seed of fear in him. Before coming to Vietnam, US Army officers had been taught that everyone in Vietnam might be a Vietcong, and fear inhabited every American soldier. Every child, every mother, every monk, could be a guerilla agent. The soldiers had been educated in this way and they saw potential enemies everywhere. I had tried to express my sympathy to him. But as he heard the word, "Vietcong" he was overcome by fear and touched his gun.

I knew that I had to be very calm. I practiced breathing in and breathing out very deeply. Calmly I said: "No, I am waiting for my plane to go to Da Nang so I can assess the situation of the flooding there." By sitting very still and talking in a very calm voice, I hoped to convey that I had a lot of sympathy for him and the fact that the war had created a lot of victims, not only among the Vietnamese but also among the Americans. Fortunately, I had enough serenity that he reestablished his calm and released his grip on the gun. If I had acted out of fear, he might have shot me out of his fear. By my taking care and speaking in a mindful way, both of us were able to continue on our journey, with a little more understanding between us.

Danger often comes from the inside. Some accidents are not preventable, but if you are stable and clear enough, there are times when you can defuse and calm a potentially dangerous or fatal situation.

Heat

In Saigon in 1965, I was working on war relief and living in cramped quarters at Van Hanh University. The rooms were unbearably stuffy. The paper ceiling offered no protection from the searing heat, and by noontime we had to go for relief under the areca trees. Such extreme heat took away our appetites as well. On such days, escaping the city and being able to return to a village in the countryside was as delightful as swimming in a cool river. Feeling the breeze blowing and the sight of rice fields and palm trees was utterly refreshing.

In Saigon, a neighbor, Mr. Tu, tried to persuade me to put an air conditioner in the room where I worked. He did his best to convince me of the benefits—it would cost money, but it would allow us to accomplish twice as much work.

There was truth in that. It was impossible to write when it was so hot. Still, I decided not to purchase one. Money was not the issue; the rector had actually approved the idea and had even offered to find an inexpensive one. But we would be the only people in our poor neighborhood with an air conditioner, and that would change the way people looked at us. It is one thing to own an old car and quite another to own an air conditioner.

So I looked for another solution. Mr. Bay lived alone in a two-story house next door to the temple. He left for work every morning on his motorbike and didn't return until evening. I asked him if I could use his downstairs room during the heat of the day, and he agreed. When I wanted to write or to work undisturbed by visitors, I just went next door.

In Vietnam, friends drop by whenever they feel like it. No one telephones first or makes an appointment. By not being at home, I avoided being rude, were anyone to drop in. I did, however, spend a few hours each day working in the university office, which, because of the oppressive heat, was my least favorite activity.

Another solution to the heat was the chilled sweet soup sold by a neighborhood vendor. She made mung bean and areca flower soups, just like the ones in central Vietnam. I was fond of both kinds. In Vietnamese, sweet soup is called *che*. It is difficult to describe che to someone who has never tasted it, but it is delicious. The vendor sold them chilled. Two small bowls on a hot day were as refreshing as a tall glass of cool coconut milk.

At Sea on Solid Ground

Many years ago, I wrote four Chinese characters on a paper lampshade. These four characters can be translated as, "If you want peace, peace is with you immediately." A few years later, in 1976 in Singapore, I had the chance to put these words into practice.

I was in Singapore for a conference on "Religion and Peace," and became aware of the situation of what the government called the "boatpeople"—Vietnamese refugees who were attempting to escape persecution and violence at home. At that time, the world did not know about the boatpeople, and the governments of Thailand, Malaysia, and Singapore would not allow them to land. Singapore had a particularly harsh policy. Every time refugees in a boat tried to come ashore, they were pushed back out to sea to die.

Several of us began to organize a program to help the refugees. We called the program When Blood Is Shed, We All Suffer. We hired two large ships—the *Leapdal* and the *Roland*—to pick up refugees on the open sea, and two small ships—the *Saigon 200* and the *Blackmark*—to communicate between the shore and the boats and to transport food and supplies. Our plan was to fill the two large ships with refugees and take them to Australia and Guam, where, on arrival, we would inform the press, so that the world would take notice of their plight, and they would not be sent back. It's not enough just to talk about compassion; we have to do the work of compassion. We had to do our work in secret, since most national governments did not want to acknowledge the situation of the boatpeople at that time, and we knew we would be deported from Singapore if we were discovered.

We managed to rescue nearly eight hundred boatpeople from the Gulf of Siam. On New Year's Eve, I rowed out to sea in the small

Saigon 200 to talk with the refugees on the larger ships. Using a megaphone, I wished them a Happy New Year. After we said goodbye, I headed back to shore, and in the darkness, a huge wave suddenly welled up and drenched me. I had the impression that the great power of darkness was warning me, "It is the fate of these people to die. Why are you interfering?"

In Singapore if we wanted to help the boatpeople, we had no choice but to break the law. We went to the houses of fishermen and told them, "Any time you rescue boatpeople, please telephone us. We will come and get them so the government can't punish you for helping them." We gave them our telephone number, and from time to time a fisherman would call us, and we would go by taxi to pick up the refugee. Then we would take him or her to the French embassy, at night, when the embassy was closed, and we would help the boatperson climb into the embassy compound and tell them to wait there until morning.

The French ambassador in Singapore at that time was very compassionate. When he discovered the boatpeople in the morning, he would call the Singapore police to collect them. He knew that if he was the one passing them on, the boatpeople would get "illegal refugee" status and would be safe in prison. Being imprisoned was far better than being sent back out to sea where they would have died.

The suffering we touched doing this kind of work was so deep that if we did not have a reservoir of spiritual strength, we would not have been able to continue. During those days, we practiced sitting and walking meditation, and eating our meals in silence in a very concentrated way. We knew that without this kind of discipline, we would fail in our work. The lives of many people depended on our mindfulness practice.

Unfortunately, after we had rescued nearly eight hundred refugees from small boats at sea, the government of Singapore discovered our program to bring them to Australia on the *Roland* and the *Leapdal*. At two o'clock one morning, the Singapore police surrounded the building where I was staying. Two policemen blocked the front door, two blocked the back, and two came inside. They confiscated my travel documents and ordered me to leave the country within twenty-four hours.

At that moment, we already had eight hundred people aboard our two large ships. We had to find a way for them to get to safety somewhere on shore in Australia or Guam. What could we do? We had to breathe deeply, with full awareness. At that time of night, no one would answer the phone. We could not go back to sleep. We began to practice slow walking meditation inside our small apartment.

The *Saigon 200* and the *Blackmark* were not allowed to leave port to take food and water to the refugees aboard the *Leapdal* and the *Roland*. The *Roland* had enough fuel to reach Australia, but its engine had broken down. We needed to get food to them. The weather was very windy and the sea quite rough, and we worried about the ship's safety, even drifting off shore, but the Malaysian government would not allow it to enter Malaysian waters. I had already tried to get permission to enter a neighboring country so we could continue the rescue operation, but the governments of Thailand, Malaysia, and Indonesia would not grant me an entry visa. Then we got word that there was a child being born on one of the boats, the *Leapdal*.

Although I was on solid ground, I too was drifting out at sea, because my life was one with the eight hundred refugees on our two ships.

In this extremely difficult situation, I realized that I needed to put into practice the words "If you want peace, peace is with you immediately." I was surprised to find myself quite calm, not afraid or worried about anything. My worries had disappeared—it was truly a peaceful state of mind.

And yet there were more problems than it seemed possible to solve in just twenty-four hours. Even in a whole lifetime, many of us complain that there is not enough time. How could so much be done in a mere twenty-four hours? I vowed that if I could not have peace at that moment, I would never be able to have peace. If I could not be peaceful in the midst of danger, then the kind of peace I might have in simpler times is meaningless. If I could not find peace in the midst of difficulty, I knew I would never know real peace. As long as I live, I will never forget those seconds of sitting meditation, those breaths, and those mindful steps through the night.

Success finally came when I faced the problem directly. At four o'clock in the morning, the idea came to me to ask the French ambassador to intervene so that we could stay on in Singapore ten more days to complete the operation and bring the refugees to safety. But the French embassy didn't open until eight, so we continued our practice of walking meditation outside.

We were at the gate of the embassy when it opened at eight. We went in and talked to the ambassador, and he wrote a letter to the Singapore government, intervening in our favor and asking them to allow us to stay ten more days. As soon as we had the letter, we rushed to the Immigration Office, which sent us to the Ministry of Foreign Affairs. Right before noon, they agreed to grant us an extension. We had only fifteen minutes to get back to the Immigration Office to have our visas renewed for ten days. If we hadn't had a spiritual dimension in our lives, we would have been lost.

The Coconut Monk

During the war, there was a monk who lived on an island in the middle of the Mekong River. He built a platform in a coconut tree where he could meditate. Up there he could feel the breeze and enjoy looking down at the river. The Coconut Monk did many things in order to educate people about peace. He organized a practice center on the island and invited people to come and practice sitting meditation with him. He collected bullets and bomb fragments and made them into a big bell, a bell of mindfulness, which he hung in his practice center. Every morning and evening he invited the bell to sound. He wrote a beautiful poem in which he said:

> *Dear bullets, dear bombs,*
> *I have helped you to come together to practice.*
> *In your former life you have killed and destroyed.*
> *But in this life you are practicing,*
> *calling people to wake up,*
> *to wake up to humanity, to love, to understanding.*

Once he walked all the way to Saigon, to the presidential palace. He wanted to bring a message of peace to the president Nguyen Van Thieu. The guard wouldn't allow him to enter the palace, so he waited outside. He had carried with him a cage, and inside there was a mouse and a cat. The cat did not eat the mouse. The guard told him, "Go away; you can't keep sitting here. What is your business here?" The Coconut Monk said: "I want to show the president that even a cat and a mouse can live together peacefully."

He took care of both of them so that the cat would not feel the need to eat the mouse. He wanted to demonstrate that even a cat and a mouse can live in peace, so why not we humans? This is the kind of thing the Coconut Monk would do. Some people might think of him as crazy. It's not true. He was very lucid. Everything he did was for the purpose of getting his message across.

Mindfulness in the Battle Zone

In 1968 I went to the United States to call for cessation of the US bombing in Vietnam. In May of that year, the bombing of Saigon had become so fierce that the whole area around the campus of the School of Youth for Social Service had been destroyed. More than ten thousand refugees came to our campus, many of them wounded, and we had to take care of them. We were not at all equipped for this in terms of food, basic hygiene, or medical supplies, and it was very dangerous to travel outside the campus to get provisions. When we had used up our supply of bandages, the young women tore up their long dresses in order to make more bandages.

In this desperate situation, we had to evacuate the seriously wounded from our campus. But to do so, we had to cross the battle zone to bring them to the hospital. We decided to use the five-colored Buddhist flag to replace the Red Cross flag. The monks and nuns put on their *sanghati*s, their monastic ceremonial robes, and carried out the wounded. The Buddhist flag and the sanghati robes signaled that we were a peaceful group. Fortunately it worked, and we were able to evacuate the patients; otherwise, many would have died.

On the third day of the bombing, panic broke out in our over-crowded campus: there was a rumor that the anti-Communists were going to bomb the school because there were so many Communists among the refugees. When people heard this, many started to collect their belongings and leave, but the bombing was so heavy they were driven back. The Communists and the anti-Communists were fighting at the very edge of our campus. At that moment, Thay Thanh Van, a twenty-five-year-old monk and the school's director, took a large megaphone and was about to announce that people should not leave when he suddenly asked himself, "What if the bombing really does take place?" Thousands of people would die, and how could he, a young monk, bear such a responsibility? So he slowly put down the megaphone and did not make the announcement.

Thay Thanh Van realized that he needed to speak to both the warring parties. To do this, he had to crawl across the firing zone in order to avoid being shot by either side. First, he went to the anti-Communists and persuaded the commanding officer to instruct their planes not to bomb the campus filled with refugees. Then he went to the Communist guerrillas, who had set up antiaircraft guns right at the corner of our campus. He asked them not to shoot at enemy planes; otherwise the campus would be bombed in retaliation. Both sides were moved by his request and did as he asked. It was a miracle. On this mission he did not carry anything with him except his courage, love, and compassion.

In a situation like that, you have to be extremely mindful. Sometimes you have to react quickly while remaining calm. If you are angry or suspicious, you cannot do it. You have to be clear-minded. In the context of war, we grew deeper in our practice of nonviolence. Nonviolence is not a set of techniques that you can learn with your intellect. Nonviolent action naturally arises from the compassion, lucidity, and understanding you have within.

The Petition

During the war in Vietnam, one of my closest students, Sister Chan Khong, wrote a petition for peace. She was a professor at a university in Saigon, and she persuaded seventy of her fellow teachers to sign the petition. Shortly afterward there were widespread attacks on South Vietnam by troops from the North. The atmosphere became very tense. As a result, the local authorities made a public broadcast calling all the professors who had signed the petition to come to the Ministry of Education to sign a statement recanting their support for the peace petition. All the professors except Sister Chan Khong complied.

She was called in to speak with the minister of education himself, who said that if she did not withdraw her statement for peace, she would lose her position at the university and possibly be put in jail. Sister Chan Khong was determined to bear all responsibility for her act of initiating the petition.

Then she said, "Mr. Minister, as a teacher, I believe the most important thing we can do during this time of killing and confusion is to speak out with courage, understanding, and love. That is a precious gift that we can give to our students. That is what I did. You, the minister of education, were a teacher too, before having a high position in the government. You are like a big brother to us younger teachers." When he heard this, the minister's heart softened. He apologized and did not take any more action against Sister Chan Khong.

It is possible to water the seed of compassion even in such a situation of adversity. When we see clearly with the eyes of understanding and compassion, we no longer feel that we are the victims of violence. We can even open the heart and the eyes of the person we feel is trying to hurt us. We can turn our enemies into friends.

Martin Luther King Jr., Bodhisattva

I first wrote to Dr. King on June 1, 1965, explaining to him why some of us in Vietnam had immolated ourselves in protest against the war. I explained that it was not an act of suicide, or of despair; it was an act of love.

There are times when we have no other way than to burn ourselves in order to be heard, in order to get the message across. The people of Vietnam did not want the war, but there was no way for this voice to be heard. The warring parties controlled all the radio, television, and newspapers. To burn ourselves like that was not an act of violence. It was an act of compassion, an act of peace. The suffering of the monk who burns himself to convey a message of love and compassion—is of the same nature as the act of Jesus Christ dying on the cross, dying with no hate, no anger, only with compassion, leaving behind a compassionate call for peace, for brotherhood.

A year later, on June 1, 1966, I met the Reverend Martin Luther King Jr. in person for the first time in Chicago. From the first moment, I knew I was in the presence of a holy person. Not just his good work but his very being was a source of great inspiration for me. When those who represent a spiritual tradition embody the essence of their tradition, just the way they walk, sit, and smile speaks volumes about the tradition. Martin Luther King Jr. was young at that time, as was I. We both belonged to the Fellowship of Reconciliation, an organization working to help groups in conflict find peaceful resolution.

We had tea together in his room, and then we went down for a press conference. In the press conference, Dr. King spoke out for the first time against the Vietnam War. That was the day we combined our efforts to work for peace in Vietnam and to fight for civil rights in the US. We agreed that the true enemy of man is not man. Our enemy is not outside of us. Our true enemy is the anger, hatred, and discrimination that is found in the hearts and minds of man. We have to identify the real enemy and seek nonviolent ways to remove it. I told the press that his activities for civil rights and human rights were perfectly in accord with our efforts in Vietnam to stop the war.

In May 1967, one year later, I met Martin Luther King Jr. again in Geneva at a conference called *Pacem in Terris*—"Peace on Earth"— organized by the World Council of Churches. Dr. King was staying on the eleventh floor; I was on the fourth floor. He invited me up for breakfast. On my way, I was detained by the press, so I arrived late. He had kept the breakfast warm for me and had waited for me. I greeted him, "Dr. King, Dr. King!"

"Dr. Hanh, Dr. Hanh!" he replied.

We were able to continue our discussion on peace, freedom, and community, and what kind of steps America could take to end the war. And we agreed that without a community, we cannot go very far. Without a happy, harmonious community, we will not be able to realize our dream.

I said to him, "Martin, do you know something? In Vietnam they call you a bodhisattva, an enlightened being trying to awaken other living beings and help them move toward more compassion and understanding." I'm glad I had the chance to tell him that, because just a few months later he was assassinated in Memphis.

I was in New York when I heard the news of his assassination; I was devastated. I could not eat; I could not sleep. I made a deep vow to continue building what he called "the beloved community," not only for myself but for him also. I have done what I promised to Martin Luther King Jr. And I think that I have always felt his support.

Prisoner of Conscience

I know a Buddhist nun who had graduated from Indiana University in the US and who was practicing in Vietnam. She was arrested by the police and put into prison because of her actions for peace and reconciliation. She tried her best to practice in her prison cell. It was difficult, because during the daytime if they saw her practice sitting meditation in her cell, they considered it an act of provocation and defiance to be sitting like that, experiencing peace. So they forbade her from sitting in meditation. She would have to wait until they turned off the light in order to sit up and practice. They tried to steal from her even the opportunity to practice. Yet she was able to continue. She did walking meditation, although the space she had was very small. She was also able to talk with kindness and gentleness to the people who were locked in the same cell. Thanks to her practice, she was able to help them to suffer less.

I have another Vietnamese friend who was put into a "reeducation" camp in North Vietnam, in a remote jungle area. During his four years there, he practiced meditation and was able to live with inner peace. By the time he was released, his mind was as sharp as a sword. He knew that he had not lost anything during those four years. On the contrary, he knew he had "reeducated himself in meditation."

Many things can be taken from us, but no one can ever steal our determination or our freedom. No one can ever steal our practice. Even in extreme cases, it is possible to maintain our happiness, our peace, and our inner freedom. As long as we are still able to breathe and walk and smile, we can be at peace, and we can be happy.

I'm from the Center

Once I was walking with many people in Philadelphia as part of a demonstration to stop the war in Vietnam. A reporter came up to me and asked, "Are you from the North, or are you from the South?" To him, if I was from the North, I would be anti-American, a Communist; and if I were from the South, I would be an anti-Communist. I was walking mindfully, and he was holding out the microphone. I stopped for a second, and said, "I'm from the center."

Sometimes people have a certain idea or way of looking at things, and they want to put you in a box. But what happens if you don't belong in any of the categories in their mind? It's the reality of the thing that matters, and not the word we use to describe it. A name is merely a conventional designation, it's not the reality. We must train ourselves to look deeply into the true nature of reality.

When we think of Paris, we have an idea, a view about Paris and words to describe Paris. But Paris is very different from the view and the words that we have. Perhaps we visited Paris for a few days, and so we think we know it. There are those who have lived ten or twenty years in Paris and have not discovered all the truth of the city. We shouldn't mistake the word and the idea for the truth.

One day in the late 1980's, I was on a panel in Amsterdam. A theologian stood up and asked me about a sentence in *Lotus in a Sea of Fire*, a book I'd written in 1967. I looked at him and said, "I didn't write that book." He was very shocked. But the truth was, I was a living being in front of him, and he was interested in a phantom from twenty years earlier. In 1967 the situation in Vietnam and in the world was very different. Each one of us is constantly changing. We don't need to be caught in an idea of ourselves from many years ago.

This Is Not China

While in the US in 1966, I gave a talk at a church in Minneapolis, and afterward I was very tired. I walked slowly in meditation back to my room so I could enjoy the cold, fragrant night air and be nourished and healed by it.

While I was walking mindfully, taking each step in freedom, a car came up from behind and came to a screeching halt very close to me. The driver threw open the door, glared at me, and shouted: "This is America; this is not China!" and drove off. Maybe he thought, "Who is this Chinese person who dares to walk in freedom in America," and he could not bear it. Maybe he thought, "This is America; only white people can live here. You Chinese people, how dare you come here, how dare you walk with such freedom? You have no right to walk that way. This is America; this is not China."

I was not angry—that was the good thing about it—I thought it was rather funny. I thought: "If he had just paused for a moment, I would have told him, 'I agree with you one hundred percent, this is America; this is not China; why do you have to shout at me?'"

We know that the seed of discrimination lies in all of us. I have been shouted at by all kinds of people of all different shades of color. The oppressed and the oppressors lie within each one of us, and our practice is to attain the wisdom of nondiscrimination.

When people call us African American, we should answer, "Yes." When they call us African, we answer, "Yes," and when they call us American, we also answer, "Yes." When people call the names of those who are discriminated against, we answer, "Yes." And when they call the names of those who are discriminating against others, we also answer, "Yes." All of them are us. Within each of us is both the victim of discrimination and the one who discriminates.

Alfred Hassler

My friend Alfred Hassler worked for the Fellowship of Reconciliation in Nyack, New York. Together with Professor George Kahin of Cornell University, he was responsible for bringing me to the United States to speak about the war in Vietnam. Alfred organized a tour for me to speak in a number of churches and universities around the United States in 1966.

Alfred Hassler spent a lot of time working with us to raise awareness about the suffering of the Vietnamese people in the war. Working for peace brought him a great deal of happiness and pleasure. After the tour in North America, he helped organize tours in Europe, Asia, and Australia as well. We spent a lot of time together.

One day many years later, I was about to lead a mindfulness retreat in upstate New York, when we heard that Alfred was dying in a Catholic Hospital in New York City. The hospital was not far away, so some of the nuns and monks who were close to him, including Sister Chan Khong and myself, decided to make a detour to come and see him. When we arrived at the hospital, Alfred was already in a coma. His wife Dorothy and his daughter Laura were there. They were so happy when we arrived.

Sister Chan Khong and I went up to his room. He had been in a coma for a while and did not wake up when we came in. Sister Chan Khong began to sing to him a song that I had written: "This body is not me; I am not caught in this body. I am life without boundaries. My nature is the nature of no birth and no death."

As she began to sing for the third time, Alfred regained consciousness. Don't think that when someone is in a coma, you can no longer communicate with them. Speak to them anyway. Somehow, they can perceive your message.

Sister Chan Khong began to tell stories about the times we had all worked together for peace. She retold many stories of peacemaking. "Alfred do you remember the day in Rome when three hundred Catholic priests held up the names of three hundred Buddhist monks in Vietnam who were in prison because they had refused to go into the Army? Alfred, do you remember the time we were in Copenhagen?"

She continued to talk to him about the happy experiences we'd had during the time of working for peace together. I was massaging his feet and Sister Chan Khong was recalling the memories. Suddenly Alfred opened his mouth and said, "Wonderful, wonderful." After that he sank back into the coma.

It was getting dark, and we were scheduled to give the first teaching of the retreat that evening, so we had to leave. The next morning I received the news from his daughter that Alfred had died a few hours after we left, very peacefully and without pain.

Call Me By My True Names

In the early years of my exile in France, I learned of an eleven-year-old girl escaping from Vietnam with her family and other boat people. She was raped by a pirate, right there on her boat. Her father tried to intervene, but the pirate threw her father into the sea. After the child was raped she jumped into the ocean to commit suicide. We received the news of this tragedy one day while we were working in our Buddhist Peace Delegation office in Paris. I was so upset I could not sleep. I felt anger, blame, and despair.

That evening in sitting meditation, I visualized myself being born as a baby boy into a very poor fishing family on the coast of Thailand. My father was a fisherman. He couldn't read; he had never gone to school or to the temple; he had never received any Buddhist teaching or any kind of education. The politicians, educators, and social workers in Thailand had never helped my father. My mother also couldn't read or write, and she didn't know how to raise her children. My father's family had been poor fishermen for many generations— my grandfather and my great-grandfather had been fishermen, too. When I turned thirteen, I also became a fisherman. I had never gone to school, I had never felt loved or understood, and I lived in chronic poverty that persisted from one generation to the next.

Then one day another young fisherman says to me: "Let's go out onto the ocean. There are boatpeople who pass near here and they often carry gold and jewelry, sometimes even money. Just one trip and we can be free from this poverty." I accept the invitation, thinking, "We only need to take away a little bit of their jewelry; it won't do any harm, and then we can be free from this poverty." So I become a pirate. The first time I go out, I'm not even aware that I have become a pirate. Once out on the ocean, I start to see the other pirates raping young women on the boats. I had never touched a young woman; I had never even thought about holding hands or going out with a young woman. But then on one boat there is a very beautiful young woman, and no policeman there to stop me. I had seen other people doing it, and I asked myself: "Why don't I try it, too? This is my chance to try the body of a young woman." And so I did.

If you were there on the boat and had a gun, you might have shot me. But shooting me wouldn't help me. Nobody had ever taught me how to love, how to understand, how to see the suffering of others. My father and mother were not taught this either. I didn't know what was wholesome and what was unwholesome, I didn't understand cause and effect. I was living in the dark. If you had a gun, you could shoot me, and I would die. But you wouldn't be able to help me at all.

As I continued sitting, I saw hundreds of babies being born that night along the coast of Thailand in similar circumstances, many of them baby boys. If the politicians and cultural ministers could look deeply, they would see that within twenty years those babies would become pirates. When I was able to see that, I understood the actions of the pirate. When I put myself in the situation of being born into a family that was uneducated and poor from one generation to the next, I saw that I would not be able to avoid becoming a pirate. When I saw that, my hatred vanished, and I could feel compassion for that pirate.

When I saw those babies being born and growing up with no help, I knew that I had to do something so that they would not become pirates. The energy of a bodhisattva, a compassionate being with limitless love, grew inside me. I didn't suffer anymore. I could embrace not only the suffering of the eleven-year-old child who was raped, but also the suffering of the pirate.

When you address me as "Venerable Nhat Hanh," I answer, "Yes." When you call the name of the child who was raped, I also answer, "Yes." If you call the name of the pirate, I will also say, "Yes." Depending on where I was born, and under which circumstances I grew up, I might have been the girl or I might have been the pirate.

I am the child in Uganda or the Congo, all skin and bones, my two legs as thin as bamboo sticks. And I am also the arms merchant, selling deadly weapons to the Congo. Those poor children in the Congo do not need bombs; they need food to eat. But here in the US, we live by producing bombs and guns. And if we want others to buy guns and bombs, then we have to create wars. If you call the name of the child in the Congo, I answer, "Yes." If you call the name of those who produce the bombs and guns, I also answer, "Yes." When I'm able to see that I am all those people, my hatred disappears, and I am determined to live in such a way that I can help the victims, and also help those who create and perpetrate wars and destruction.

Healing the Wounds of War

We have held many meditation retreats with Vietnam veterans in the US. They are wonderful, but they are not always easy, because many veterans are still struggling with their pain. During a retreat in the early nineties, one gentleman told me that in Vietnam he lost 417 people in one battle alone, in one day. He has had to live with that ever since.

One soldier told me that the retreat was the first time in fifteen years that he had felt safe in a group of people. For fifteen years, he had not been able to swallow solid food easily. He had stopped talking to other people. But after three or four days of practicing mindful sitting and mindful walking, he began to open up and talk to people. You have to offer a lot of loving kindness in order to help people like this touch life deeply again. During the retreat, we encouraged each other to come back to the many positive and healing elements within us and around us.

We ate our breakfast in silence. We took mindful, peaceful steps as we practiced walking meditation, touching the Earth with love and compassion. We breathed mindfully to get deeply in touch with the fresh air, and we looked deeply into our cup of tea in order to be truly in touch with the tea, the water, the clouds, and the rain. We sat together, breathed together, walked together, and tried to learn from our experience in Vietnam.

Veterans have experience that makes them the light at the tip of the candle, illuminating the roots of war and the way to peace. We can learn a lot from their suffering. Nothing exists by itself alone. We all belong to each other; we cannot cut reality into pieces. My happiness is your happiness; my suffering is your suffering. We heal and transform together. Every side is "our side"; there is no evil side, no enemy.

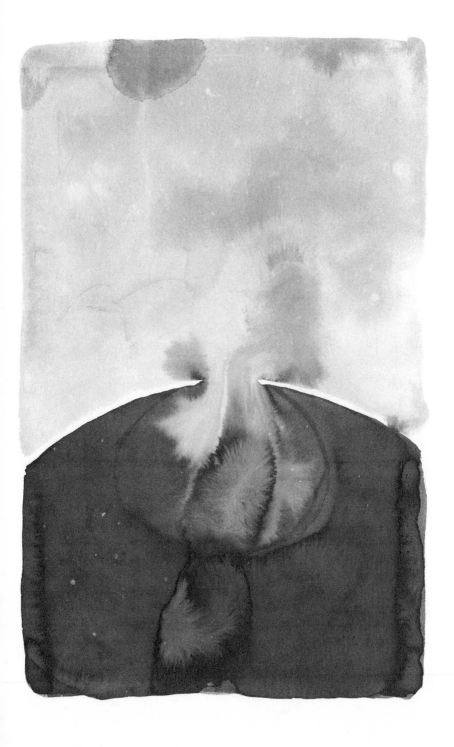

Practice Is a Boat

I met a Vietnam War veteran who had killed five innocent Vietnamese children during the war, and who could not forgive himself for having done so. His unit had been caught in an ambush and many of his friends had been killed; only he and a few others survived. He was furious. To retaliate, he set a trap in the village where his friends had been killed. He made sandwiches with meat and other things, put explosives between the pieces of bread, and left them near the entrance of the village.

Then he hid himself to observe. Soon, some children came out, discovered the sandwiches, and began to eat them. As he watched, the children begin to cry and suffer terribly. Their parents rushed out in despair. They wanted to call an ambulance, but it was a very remote place, and it was impossible. The soldier knew that even if there had been an ambulance, it would have been too late to save the children. He watched the children die in agony in their parents' arms.

Ever since he returned to the United States, he couldn't sleep. If he was ever in a room alone with children, it was unbearable, and he would rush out as quickly as possible. He could not talk about it to anyone, except his mother, who could not hear it. She said, "My dear son, that is the nature of war. Such things always happen in war. Do not blame yourself too harshly." That did not help him at all, and he continued to suffer. He could not forgive himself for having killed these five children.

He told this story at the first retreat we held for Vietnam veterans. It was a very difficult retreat. Many veterans had come to the retreat on the advice of their psychotherapists, but they were suspicious that the retreat might be a kind of ambush in order to kill them, especially as a Vietnamese Buddhist monk was conducting the retreat.

One day during walking meditation, I saw a veteran walking behind the group, following us at a distance of about twenty meters. When someone asked him why he didn't walk with us, he explained that if there was an ambush, if he stayed behind, he would still have time to run away. Another veteran could not sleep in a dormitory. He put a tent in the woods where he could sleep alone, and he set up traps around his tent in order to protect himself. Many veterans could not say a word.

One day I turned to the veteran who had killed the five children with poisoned sandwiches, and invited him to my room. "It is true you have killed five children," I said, "but it is also true that today you can save five children."

There are children dying everywhere in the world, including in the United States, due to violence, poverty, and oppression. In some cases, it would take just a little bit of medicine, food, or warm clothes to help save that child. I asked the veteran, "Why don't you use your life to save children like these? You have killed five children, but now you have the opportunity to save fifty children. In the present moment, you can heal the past."

The practice of mindfulness is like a boat, and by practicing mindfulness, you offer yourself a boat. As long as you continue to practice, as long as you stay in the boat, you will not sink or drown in the river of suffering.

The veteran slowly took in these words. He devoted his life to helping children and in the process became healed by his work. The present moment contains the past, and if you can live deeply in the present moment you can heal the past. You don't have to wait for anything.

First Blossoms

I grew up in Vietnam. I became a monk in Vietnam. I learned and practiced Buddhism in Vietnam. And before coming to the West, I taught several generations of Buddhist students in Vietnam. But I can say now that it was in the West that I realized my path.

In 1962 I was invited to teach at Princeton University, and it was there that I began to have many deep insights, flowers and fruits of the practice. For me, going to Princeton was like entering a monastery. At that time, it was an all-male university, with no female students, and I lived in Brown Hall in the Theological Seminary. The atmosphere was very peaceful and wholesome. It was so different from the intensity and pressure I had left in Vietnam. I had a lot of time to do walking meditation along the college paths. It was in Princeton that I saw my first winter snow, my first spring, and my first autumn. It was there that I truly tasted, for the first time, the peace of dwelling happily in the present moment.

Mindfulness is my basic meditation practice. Mindfulness means dwelling in the present moment and becoming aware of every-thing—both the positive and negative elements that are there both within us and around us. We learn to nourish the positive and to recognize, embrace, and transform the negative.

We can remind ourselves every day that the practice isn't about getting somewhere or achieving something. The practice itself is the very joy and peace we are seeking. The practice *is* the destina-tion. It is possible for each one of us to dwell happily in the present moment.

The Bamboo Grove

When I returned to Vietnam from the US in 1964, I was living in the busy center of Saigon. There I set up the Van Hanh Buddhist University, published the *Voice of the Rising Tide*, and prepared the ground for opening the School of Youth for Social Service. I would spend as much time as I could at the Bamboo Grove Temple (Truc Lam) in Go Vap, Gia Dinh, outside the city, to enjoy the calm and beautiful atmosphere there.

One morning in my little hut at Truc Lam, I woke up very early, around three o'clock. When I put my feet on the earthen floor, the coolness made me feel very awake. I remained in that position for almost an hour. While I looked out into the darkness, I listened to the first bells of the morning. Although I could not distinguish particular objects, I knew that the plum tree and the bamboo thicket were there. In the darkness of the night, I knew that you were there, because I was there.

You are there for me, and I am here for you; that is the teaching of interbeing. Consciousness is always consciousness of something; cognition always includes subject and object together.

The stretching arm of cognition
In a lightning flash,
Joining together a million eons of distance,
Joining together birth and death,
Joining together the knower and the known.

The Blossoming of Plum Village

Hermitage in the Wind

About thirty years ago, I was enjoying a solo retreat in the hermitage at our Sweet Potato Community in northern France, in a forest called la Forêt d'Othe. I liked sitting and walking in the woods. One very beautiful morning, I decided to spend the whole day in the woods, so I brought along a bowl of rice, some sesame seeds, a bottle of water, and off I went. I planned to stay out the whole day, but around three in the afternoon, black clouds began to gather in the sky. Before leaving the hermitage that morning, I had opened the door and all the windows so the sunshine and fresh air could come in. But soon the wind began to blow hard, and I knew I had to go back and take care of the hermitage.

On arriving home, I found the hermitage in a terrible state of disarray. Strong gusts of wind had strewn the papers from my desk all over the place. It felt miserably cold and dark. The very first thing I did was to close the door and all the windows so the wind couldn't continue to wreak havoc. Then I made a fire in the fireplace and, as the fire started to come alive, I began to collect all the sheets of paper from the floor, gathered them on the table, placed a little brick on top, and tried to make the hermitage tidy and in order. Soon the fire had made everything warm, pleasant, and cozy. I sat down by the fire, toasted my fingers, and enjoyed listening to the wind and the rain outside.

There are days when you feel it's just not your day, and that everything is going wrong. The more you try, the worse the situation becomes. Everyone has days like that. That's when it's time to stop everything, go home, and to take refuge in yourself. The first thing to do is to close the doors and windows. The eyes, ears, nose, tongue, body, and mind are the six windows you close when everything feels

like a mess. Our six senses are windows to the mind. Close everything in order to prevent the strong wind from blowing in and making
you miserable.

Shut the windows, shut the door, and make a fire. Create a feeling
of warmth, coziness, and comfort by practicing mindful breathing.
Rearrange everything—your feelings, your perceptions, your emotions—they're all scattered everywhere; it's a mess inside. Recognize
and embrace each emotion. Collect them the way I collected all the
sheets of paper that were scattered all over the hermitage. Practice
mindfulness and concentration, and tidy up everything within yourself. This will help you restore your calm and peace.

If we only rely on external conditions, we will get lost. We need
a refuge we can always rely on, and that is the island of self. Firmly
established on our inner island, we're very safe. We can take time
to recover and restore ourselves, and become stronger, until we're
ready to go out again and engage.

Even if you are very young, you can find that island within
yourself. Every time you suffer badly, and nothing seems to be
going right, stop everything and go to that island right away. Take
refuge in your inner island for as long as you need. It may be five,
ten, fifteen minutes, or half an hour. You will feel stronger and much
better within.

Enjoy Your Sleeping Bag

In 1969, at the request of the Unified Buddhist Church in Vietnam, I helped set up the Buddhist Peace Delegation at the Paris Peace Talks. It was my third year in exile, and I had sought asylum in France. The talks were already underway, but the voice of the people of Vietnam, who wanted peace and an end to war, was not being heard.

The headquarters for the Buddhist Peace Delegation in Paris was a very small apartment in a poor Arab quarter. Many people were staying there together, and it was so crowded that on occasion Sister Chan Khong had to ask to sleep overnight in a local restaurant because there was not enough floor space left.

It was a challenge to find enough food to eat and clothing to wear. Instead of buying regular rice at a supermarket, we would buy the cheaper broken rice, usually sold as bird feed, from the pet store. One day the man who was selling the broken rice asked us, "Why do you buy so much rice? You must have a lot of birds in your house." We said, "Yes, there are nine in all, and each one is very big!" And we gestured with our hands to show just how big those birds were.

Despite the hardships, our life was full of happiness. I found a place to teach, and I received one thousand French francs as salary every month. Other people in the delegation also had to find work. Sister Chan Khong, who had been a professor at a university in Saigon, taught mathematics and tutored young students to supplement our income. I took a course on printing as a trade. We had a printing machine and produced books for refugees to help relieve their suffering and to help them learn a foreign language so that they could settle in other countries.

Ten years later, we found land in the southwest of France and founded Plum Village Mindfulness Practice Center. I never wanted to build a luxurious, beautiful monastery. Whatever money we were offered we would send to Vietnam to bring relief to the hungry and to victims of floods. There are still many people who visit Plum Village and sleep in sleeping bags. To this day, Sister Chan Khong still sleeps in a sleeping bag. I used to sleep on a very thin foam mattress on a plank of wood on top of four bricks, one under each corner. Sleeping in sleeping bags on planks of wood did not prevent us from being happy.

The Peugeot

In the 1970s, within a few years of arriving in France, our group
bought a little car, a secondhand Peugeot. We went all over Europe
in it, and used the car to transport, not only people, but sand, bricks,
tools, books, food, and many other materials as we began to establish the Sweet Potato Community in an old farmhouse outside Paris.
We used it for all our needs and kept it for many years. When our
car was old and couldn't be used anymore, we had a difficult time
letting it go. We were attached to our little Peugeot, because both
we and the car had gone through so much together. It had survived
breakdowns, numerous accidents, and untold repairs. My friends and
I were sad the night we had to abandon it.

I do not know if people develop such a deep connection to the
things they buy these days. Many people have a strong desire to
possess the latest thing, and manufacturers and advertisers know
this. It is not by accident that merchandise these days is not created
to last.

The objects of our desire are constantly changing. And our
desires for the objects we consume also change from one moment
to the next. We are always running after something new. We may be
infatuated with what we've bought for a while, but soon we take it for
granted, we get bored, throw it away, and then buy something else.

As you grow in mindfulness, you reclaim your life. You begin to
see how much time we lose in empty, meaningless consumption.
Looking deeply, we see that empty consumption brings us no lasting
happiness, only suffering.

Mr. Mounet and the Cedar Trees

The first property we purchased for Plum Village was an old farm with about fifty-two acres of cultivated land and forty-eight acres of forest, as well as a number of stone buildings: a large barn, stables, and storehouses.

We planted 1,250 plum trees, the money for which was donated by the children who came to practice at our center. That is the reason we named our center Plum Village. Many children saved their pocket money in order to buy plum trees. It cost thirty-five French francs to plant a baby plum tree. We planted 1,250 trees because that was the number of monastics in the Buddha's original Sangha. We planned to dry the plums to make prunes and also to make plum jam—all of which we would sell so that we could send the proceeds to hungry children in Vietnam. There were only a few of us monastics there at that time, and we were looking after a number of Vietnamese refugees who were very weak from their ordeals in the war and their journey to France. It was a lot of work to renovate the dilapidated property and make it inhabitable. An enormous amount of physical labor was required, and we also had to learn how to farm in a climate very different from that of our native land.

We were blessed in having a neighbor who was a true bodhisattva, Mr. Mounet. The house he lived in was the original main house of the farmstead and was situated very close to us. He helped us a tremendous amount, lending us his tools, showing us what to plant and when, and he was always cheerful no matter what happened. Mr. Mounet was a big man and very strong. We depended on him, and we loved him very much.

One day I was shocked to hear that he had died of a heart attack, with no warning. We took a lot of care to prepare his funeral and

to send our spiritual support and energy to him. One night I felt so pained by the loss of our friend that I could not sleep. As I was doing walking meditation to ease the sadness I felt at his death, the image of Mr. Mounet came up in my mind. It was Mr. Mounet certainly, but not Mr. Mounet as I had known him. It was Mr. Mounet as a child, smiling the smile of the Buddha, happy and calm. It was Mr. Mounet's goodness smiling at me, still alive within me.

The loss of a friend like Mr. Mounet was so painful. I had to deliver a talk the next morning. I wanted to sleep but I coudn't, so I practiced breathing. It was a cold winter night, and I lay in bed visualizing the beautiful trees in the yard of my hermitage.

Years before, I had planted three beautiful cedars, a variety from the Himalayas. The trees are now very big, and during walking meditation, I used to stop and hug these beautiful cedars, breathing in and out. The cedars always responded to my hugging, I am sure of it. So I lay in bed, and just breathed in and out, becoming the cedars and my breath. I felt much better, but I still couldn't sleep.

Finally I imagined a delightful Vietnamese child nicknamed Little Bamboo. She came to Plum Village when she was two years old, and she was so cute that everyone wanted to hold her in their arms, especially the children. They barely let Little Bamboo walk on the ground! She was now six years old. I practiced breathing and smiling with her image. In just a few moments, I fell sound asleep.

Each of us needs a reserve of memories and experiences that are beautiful, healthy, and strong enough to help us during difficult moments. Sometimes when the pain in us is so big, we cannot truly touch life's wonders. We need help. But if we have a strong storehouse of happy memories and experiences, we can bring them to mind to help us embrace the block of pain inside.

You may have a friend who is very close to you and who understands you deeply. Just being with them, without saying anything is already a great comfort. In difficult moments you can invite the image of your friend to come up into your consciousness, and the two of you can breathe together. You will feel better right away.

Whenever you are with your friend, you are able to reestablish the balance within you. That is why when you are sitting or walking with them, you need to practice mindfulness so that you experience their presence deeply. This will help you to find your inner strength in order to feel solid when you are alone again. But if you just use your friend's presence to ease your suffering, the memory of them will not be strong enough to sustain you when you return home. Every positive experience we live deeply, in full awareness, is like a wholesome seed planted in our consciousness. We need to practice mindfulness all the time so that we can plant healing, positive seeds in ourselves. Then, when we need them, they will be able to take care of us.

Umbrella Pines

We held our very first summer retreat for families at the Sweet Potato Hermitage in the north of France. However, it was such a small center that it did not have enough space for everyone. So we came to the south to look for land and establish a practice center that could hold more people.

When we first saw the Upper Hamlet, I liked it immediately because it was beautiful. I saw the path that we could use for our walking meditation, and I fell in love with it at first sight. However, Mr. Dezon, the landowner, did not want to sell the property. He loved that piece of land very much, and he had been a farmer there for a long time.

We continued looking for land, and a few days later, on September 28, 1982, we found the Lower Hamlet and purchased it. But we still wanted the Upper Hamlet, so we continued to pay attention to what was going on up there. That year there was a hailstorm that destroyed all the vineyards on Mr. Dezon's property. He got angry and put the land on the market for a very high price, not really intending to sell it. In spite of the increased price, we bought it because we liked the land so much.

Anh Thieu came from Vietnam by boat with his wife and two children. They were the first people to help us start Plum Village. From the winter of 1982 to the summer of 1983, we had to work a lot. In early 1983, we began to plant some trees in the Upper Hamlet. The first trees were six umbrella pine trees. The land in the Upper Hamlet was full of rocks, so we needed the help of a local farmer and his machine to dig holes for the trees. We put a little cow manure in the bottom of each hole. It was raining that day, and everybody was soaked. Afterward I got sick and stayed in bed for three weeks.

Everybody was worried. Fortunately, after a while, I could get up and eat some rice soup.

In those days, we called our new home Persimmon Village. In the 1950s, we had the Fragrant Palm Leaves Community in the Dao Lai forest in the Central Highlands of Vietnam, but the School of Youth for Social Service needed a center closer to the city. When I wrote the book *The Miracle of Mindfulness*, I mentioned the idea of founding a practice center called Persimmon Village. Eight years later, our vision came true. We thought of planting persimmons, but we realized it was not practical, so we planted plum trees instead. We were naive, thinking that, if we planted many plum trees, we could make enough income to support ourselves. We were not horticulturists, so we did not do very well. We have enjoyed more plum blossoms than plums. The name Plum Village was beautiful, so we changed the name from Persimmon Village to Plum Village.

Binding Books

In the early years of Plum Village, I really enjoyed binding books.
It was a simple method. Using a toothbrush, a small wheel, and a
four- or five-pound fire-proof brick, I could usually bind two books
a day. Before binding I would gather all the pages and arrange them
numerically around several long planks of wood. Then I would walk
up and down the lines, and when I'd walked all the way around, I
would know that I had the correct number of pages for one signa-
ture. As I walked, I knew that I wasn't going anywhere in particular,
so I would walk slowly, gathering each page, conscious of each
movement, breathing softly, conscious of each breath. I was at peace
while assembling the pages, gluing them, and putting the covers on
the books.

I knew I couldn't produce as many books in a day as a profes-
sional bookbinder or a machine, but I also knew that I loved my
work. If you want to have a lot of money, you have to work hard
and quickly, but if you live simply, you can work gently and in full
awareness.

What would it take for you to enjoy your work?

Apple Juice and Pinecones

One day four children were playing at our Sweet Potatoes Community outside Paris. One was Thanh Thuy, who was not yet four and a half. The other three were her friends from school. Thuy was staying with us for several months while her father looked for a job in Paris. The four children ran off to play on the hillside behind the house and were gone for about an hour. When they returned to ask for something to drink, I took our last bottle of homemade apple juice and gave them each a full glass, serving Thuy last. Since her juice was from the bottom of the bottle, it had some pulp in it. When she noticed the particles, she pouted and refused to drink it. So the four children went back to their games on the hillside. Thuy had not drunk anything.

Half an hour later, while I was meditating in my room, I heard her calling. Thuy wanted to get herself a glass of cold water, but even on tiptoes she couldn't reach the faucet. I reminded her of the glass of juice on the table and asked her to drink that first. Turning to look at it, she saw that the pulp had settled and the juice looked clear and delicious. She went to the table and took the glass with both hands. After drinking half of it, she put it down and asked, "Is this a different glass of juice, Uncle Monk?" *Uncle Monk* is a common nickname Vietnamese children use when addressing an older monk.

"No," I answered. "It's the same one as before. It sat quietly for a bit, and now it's clear and delicious." Thuy looked at the glass again. "It really is good. Was it meditating like you, Uncle Monk?" I laughed and patted her head. "Let's say that I imitate the apple juice when I sit; that is closer to the truth."

Without a doubt, Thuy thought that the apple juice was sitting for a while to clear itself, just like her Uncle Monk. I think that Thuy, not yet four and a half, had understood the meaning of meditation without any explanation. The apple juice became clear after resting awhile. In the same way, if we rest in meditation awhile, we too become clear. This clarity refreshes us and gives us strength and serenity. When we feel refreshed, our surroundings also become refreshed.

That night, after the children had gone to sleep, a guest came. I filled a glass with the very last of the apple juice and put it on the table in the middle of the meditation room. I invited my friend to sit very quietly, just like the apple juice.

Another time, when there was a school holiday, Thuy and I took a walk and collected pinecones. She told me that the earth gives birth to pinecones so we can use them to start fires to keep warm in winter. I told her that pinecones are there to give birth to baby pine trees, not for lighting fires. Rather than being disappointed by my explanation, her eyes got even brighter.

The Happiness of Writing

During the first few years of Plum Village, I often stayed in a room in the Upper Hamlet, in the monks' living area. The room was on the first floor of the stone building, above what was then the bookstore.

At that time I was also writing the book *Old Path White Clouds*. We did not have central heating yet. There was only a woodstove in the little room above the bookstore, and the weather was very cold. I wrote with my right hand, and I put my left hand out over the stove. I was very happy writing. From time to time, I would stand up and make myself a cup of tea. The few hours I spent writing every day were like sitting with the Buddha for a cup of tea. I knew that the readers would be very happy reading the book because I had so much happiness while writing it.

Writing *Old Path White Clouds* was not hard work; rather it was an immense joy and a time of discovery. Some sections were more difficult to write than others. One difficult section was when the Buddha first gave teachings to the three Kashyapa brothers who became his disciples. Some accounts say the Buddha had to use miracles to convince them, but I wanted to show that he did it with his great compassion and understanding. The Buddha's capacity of understanding and compassion was boundless, so why would he need to use miraculous powers? I had a strong faith that I would be able to write the chapter in that light. That was the most difficult chapter for me.

The second most difficult chapter was when the Buddha went back to visit his family after his enlightenment. Although now he was an enlightened being, he was still the son of his parents and a brother to his siblings. I wished to write in a way that would retain his human qualities. The way he took his father's hand upon their meeting, the way he related to his younger sister, with his former wife Yasodhara, and his son Rahula, was all very natural. I could only write the way I did because I felt the ancestral teachers supporting me. The aim of *Old Path White Clouds* is to help readers rediscover the Buddha as a human being. I tried to sweep away the mystic halos people often ascribe to the Buddha. If we can't see the Buddha as a human being, it is difficult to feel close to and understand the Buddha.

Lotus Tea

Years ago in Vietnam, people used to go out onto a lotus pond with a small boat to put some tea leaves into an open lotus flower. The flower would close in the evening and perfume the tea during the night. Then, in the peace of early morning, when the dew was still glistening on the large lotus leaves, they would return in the boat with their friends to collect the tea. On the boat, they would take everything they needed to make delicious, fragrant tea: fresh water, a stove to heat it, teacups, and a teapot. Then in the beautiful early light of dawn, they would prepare the tea right there, enjoying the morning and drinking tea on the lotus pond. Nowadays we may have a lotus pond, but we do not seem to have the time to stop and look at it, let alone to enjoy it by making and drinking tea in that way.

In Plum Village we often have tea meditations. These tea meditations are a remnant of the times when we used to spend two or three hours just drinking a cup of tea. We take time to prepare everything beforehand so that we can enjoy a quiet and peaceful atmosphere. We arrange cushions and mats in a circle, and prepare a beautiful vase of flowers and some candles in the center. Then we come together to enjoy a cup of tea, a cookie, and the company of others for about an hour and a half. We have nothing to do and nowhere to go. In the serene, intimate, and informal atmosphere, we share poems, songs, and stories. Usually, it only takes a few minutes to drink a cup of tea, but in taking time to be truly present for one another like this, we nourish mutual understanding and happiness.

Brother and Sister

There was a young boy who used to come to Plum Village every summer with his little sister. Every time he fell over and hurt himself, instead of coming to help him, his father would shout at him. The boy vowed that when he grew up, he would never be like his father. He vowed that if he ever had children and one of them fell down and hurt themself, he wouldn't shout at them; he would try to help them. That was his firm determination.

Then one summer when they were at Plum Village, the little boy's younger sister was playing with another girl on a hammock, when the hammock broke. She fell and her knee was bleeding. The boy found himself becoming very angry, and he just wanted to yell: "It's your own fault! How could you be so stupid?"

Because he had been practicing simply noticing his feelings, without acting them out, he stopped himself from shouting. Instead, he turned around and practiced slow walking. As he walked, he recognized that the energy of anger he was feeling had been transmitted to him by his father. If he didn't practice breathing mindfully and sitting calmly and peacefully, he was going to become exactly like his father. In Sanskrit this is called *samsara*, the habitual continuation of negative or destructive behavior. The boy had a sudden urge to go home and invite his father to practice sitting meditation with him. When that good intention arose in him, all his anger and resentment toward his father began to dissolve.

The boy was only twelve years old. For a person of any age, but particularly for a twelve-year-old, it is a remarkable achievement to have an insight that transforms our afflictions. If he is capable of it, we certainly are as well.

The Linden Tree

In Plum Village, we have a beautiful linden tree that provides shade and joy to hundreds of visitors every summer. Once, during a big storm, many of its branches were broken off and the tree almost died. When I saw the linden tree after the storm, I wanted to cry. I felt the need to touch the trunk, but it hurt to do so, because I could feel that the tree was suffering. So I resolved to find ways to help it. Fortunately, I had a friend who was a tree doctor. He took such good care of the linden tree that now it is even stronger and more beautiful than before. Our home would not be the same without that tree. Whenever I can, I touch its bark and feel it deeply.

Trees are like our older brothers and sisters. We need to take care of them and treat them with great respect. Be as loyal to them as you would be to your dearest friends and family members.

Learning to Hug

The first time I learned hugging was in Atlanta in 1966. A woman poet took me to the airport and then, before saying goodbye, asked, "Is it all right to hug a Buddhist monk?" In my country, we are not used to expressing ourselves that way in public, but I thought, "I am a Zen teacher; it should be no problem for me to hug her." So I said, "Why not?" and she hugged me; but I was rather stiff. While on the plane, I decided that if I wanted to work with friends in the West, I would have to learn the culture of the West. That is why I invented hugging meditation.

Hugging meditation is a combination of East and West. It's like tea bags. Tea comes from Asia, where we harvest and steep the tea carefully. When tea came to the West, people made tea bags, which are quick and practical.

According to the practice, you have to really hug the person you are hugging. You have to make the person very real in your arms. You don't do it just for the sake of appearance, patting the person on the back two or three times to pretend you are there. Instead, be really there, fully present. Breathe consciously while hugging, and hug with all your mind, body, and heart. "Breathing in, I know my dear one is in my arms, alive. Breathing out, he is so precious to me." While you hold him and breathe in and out three times, the person in your arms becomes real, and you become real at the same time. When you love someone, you want him to be happy. If he is not happy, there is no way you can be happy. Happiness is not an individual matter. True love requires deep understanding. In fact, love is another name for understanding. If you do not understand, you cannot love properly. Without understanding, your love will only cause the other person to suffer.

Nails

I remember one day I went with a group of children to a supermarket. We were trying to make a table, and we decided to go out
together to buy a few nails. Before going to the supermarket, I told
them, "This is a session of meditation." The children were very happy
to go out on this special expedition. We agreed that we would not
buy anything other than the few nails we needed.

I led the children as we walked slowly and mindfully up and down
each aisle of the supermarket, taking time to visit all the items in the
store. Our intention was not to buy more things, but to look deeply.
From time to time we would stop, and I would point to certain items
on the shelves and explain what they contained, what had been
involved in their production, and what the effect would be of consuming them.

We can take opportunities like this to explain to our children why
we should not consume certain products, so they can learn how to
take care of themselves, take care of each other, and take care of the
Earth. There are items in the supermarket that have been made by
child labor, by children who do not have a chance to go to school.
There are items that are very toxic and destructive to produce. We
have to learn how to consume in such a way that compassion can
be maintained in our hearts. Practicing mindful consumption, we are
able to heal ourselves, heal our society, and heal the Earth.

That day with the children, we spent an hour and a half in the
supermarket. And the only thing we bought was a handful of nails.

Tangerine Meditation

Many years ago, I met a young American named Jim who asked me to teach him about the practice of mindfulness. One time when we were together, I offered him a tangerine. Jim accepted the tangerine, but he continued talking about the many projects he was involved in—his work for peace, social justice, and so on. He was eating, but at the same time he was thinking and talking. I was there with him as he peeled the tangerine and tossed the sections of it into his mouth, quickly chewing and swallowing.

Finally I said to him, "Jim, stop!" He looked at me, and I said, "Eat your tangerine." He understood. So he stopped talking, and he began to eat much more slowly and mindfully. He separated each of the remaining sections of the tangerine carefully, smelled their beautiful fragrance, put one section at a time into his mouth, and felt the juices surrounding his tongue. Tasting and eating the tangerine this way took several minutes, but he knew there was no reason to hurry, and that he had enough time to enjoy eating the tangerine. Eating this way, he knew that the tangerine had become real, the one eating the tangerine had become real, and life had also become real in that moment. What is the purpose of eating a tangerine? It is just for eating the tangerine. During the time you eat a tangerine, eating the tangerine is the most important thing in your life.

The next time you're at work or school and you have a snack like a tangerine, please put it in the palm of your hand and look at it in a way that makes the tangerine real. You don't need a lot of time to do this, just two or three seconds. Looking at it, you can see a beautiful tree, a blossom, the sunshine, and the rain, and you can see a tiny fruit forming. You can see the continuation of the sunshine and the rain, and the transformation of the baby fruit into the fully developed tangerine in your hand. You can see the color changing from green to orange, and you can see the tangerine ripening and sweetening. Looking at a tangerine in this way, you will see that everything in the cosmos is in it—the sunshine, rain, clouds, trees, leaves, everything. Peeling the tangerine, smelling it, and tasting it, you can be very happy.

Raking Leaves

In autumn I like to rake the leaves at my hermitage at Plum Village. I do it every three days or so, using a rake. I know that raking the leaves is in part to have a clean path to walk along and, if I am able, to do running meditation. When I am healthy, I like to jog at least twice a day. I practice mindful jogging and mindful raking.

But raking the leaves is not simply to have a clean path to jog or walk along: raking the leaves is just to enjoy raking the leaves. So I hold the rake in such a way that makes me feel happy, peaceful, and solid during the whole time of raking. I want to ensure every movement is an act of enlightenment, an act of joy, and an act of peace. So I am not in a hurry, because I see that the very act of raking is at least as wonderful as having a clean path. I would not be satisfied with any less than that. Every stroke I make should bring me joy, solidity, and freedom. I should be entirely myself, entirely present while raking the leaves. Then, raking the leaves is no longer just a means to arrive at an end that we call "having a clean path." Raking the leaves is life itself.

It doesn't take long to attain the fruits of the practice of raking leaves. If you can make one stroke in such a way that you are fully invested in the act of raking the leaves, then you will be rewarded right away. Each stroke is a work of art.

Breathing and Scything

Have you ever cut grass with a scythe? Many years ago, I brought a scythe home and tried to cut the grass around my hermitage. It took me over a week to find the best way to use it. The way you stand, the way you hold the scythe, and the angle of the blade on the grass are all important. I found that if I coordinated the movement of my arms with the rhythm of my breathing and worked unhurriedly while maintaining awareness of my movements, I was able to work for a longer period of time. When I didn't do this, I became tired in just ten minutes.

One day a Frenchman who had been raised in rural Italy came by to visit my neighbor. I asked him to show me how to use a scythe. He was much more adept than I, but for the most part he used the same position and movements. What surprised me was that he, too, coordinated his movements with his breathing. After that, whenever I saw a neighbor cutting his grass with a scythe, I knew he was practicing mindfulness.

Now, when using any tool, whether it is a pick, a shovel, or a rake, I coordinate my breath and my movements. Strenuous work, like moving boulders or pushing full wheelbarrows, is difficult to do with full awareness of the breath. But most garden jobs—turning the soil, making furrows, sowing seeds, spreading manure, watering—can be done in a relaxed and mindful way.

During the past few years, I have avoided tiring myself out or losing my breath. I think it is better not to mistreat my body. I must take care of it and treat it with respect, just as a musician takes care of his instrument. Applying "nonviolence" to your body is not merely a means to practice mindfulness; it is a practice in itself. Your body is not only the temple; it is also the sage.

The Mathematics Teacher

There was a mathematics teacher from Canada who came to several meditation retreats with us at Plum Village. Although he was an excellent math teacher, for many years he had been having a difficult time in his classroom because he would easily get angry. When upset, he would shout or even throw chalk at his students when they upset him. Sometimes in fits of irritation he would write comments on their homework such as "How can you be so stupid?"

After he had been practicing mindfulness for some time, he transformed dramatically. He entered the classroom in slow walking meditation. He went over to the blackboard and erased everything in an extremely gentle way. His surprised students asked, "Teacher, what's the matter? Are you sick?" He replied with a smile: "No, I'm not sick, I'm just trying to do things mindfully."

Since they didn't have a bell, he proposed that every fifteen minutes a student would clap his hands so that the entire class could stop and practice breathing, relaxing, and smiling. His students enjoyed practicing with him and grew to love him more and more. Instead of writing on their work, "How can you be so stupid?" he now wrote, "You haven't understood; it's my fault." He was now a mindful teacher and a mindfulness teacher.

His class became one of the most popular and enjoyable classes at the school. Soon every class in the school adopted his techniques. When he reached retirement age, he was so appreciated that he was asked to stay on for a few more years.

Slowly, with mindful action, we can transform ourselves, our family, our school, our workplace, our neighborhood, city hall, national government, and the global community. If you are a school-teacher, a parent, a journalist, a therapist, or a writer, use your talent to promote this change. We should practice meditation collectively, because looking deeply into our situation is no longer an individual matter. We have to combine our individual insights to create collective wisdom.

A Palm Tree in My Garden

Once when I was visiting China with a group of my students, a Zen master showed us his temple garden. Pointing at a bush he said, "When people today look at leaves and flowers, it's as if they're in a dream." Whenever I walk, especially if I'm walking in the woods, I practice being in touch with the plants and trees in such a way that they are real and not a dream. And I have succeeded! One night I had a dream in which I was practicing walking meditation among palm trees, and the young palm leaves were fresh, tender, and so green. The plants and trees seemed so real. In my dream, I stretched my hands out and touched the young palm leaves with mindfulness, appreciating their exquisite beauty. If you practice mindfulness well enough, then even in your dreams you can be mindful and touch the wonders of life. When I woke up, I told myself that as soon as I arrived back in France, I would plant a palm tree in my garden.

When I returned home, I went to a nursery and found a very beautiful young palm tree and invited her to come home to my garden. We can say that this palm tree has not only come from the nursery, but also from my dream. I planted the tree where I could see it from my window, and in spring it offers beautiful flowers. Whenever I take a break from writing or editing, I look out and see it. It is part of my Sangha, reminding me to be happy, to enjoy every moment of daily life.

Every village, neighborhood, or community should have a little park, a beautiful, calm, tranquil place where families can come and sit with other families and offer each other peace and quiet. In that park, you could plant trees that you would like to enjoy and take care of, just like I enjoy and take care of my little palm tree. Together, with other people in the neighborhood, you can take good care of the park and make the trees your friends. You can arrange a beautiful walking meditation path with places where people can sit down and just sit without having to talk or do anything. If you know the way to sit quietly, you'll be happy enough.

Don't miss the opportunities you have to sit down, without having to worry or think about doing anything. Lay down your burdens, your worries, and your projects. Just sit and feel that you are alive. Sit with your son, your daughter, your partner, your friend. That's enough to be happy.

I Am in Love

Every morning in winter when I wake up, I put on some warm clothes and go out to take a walk around the Upper Hamlet. It is usually still dark outside, and I walk gently, in touch with the nature all around me, the sky, the moon, and the stars. One time, after walking, I came back to my hut and wrote this sentence: "I am in love with Mother Earth." I was as excited as a young man who had fallen in love. My heart was beating with excitement. It is true—as soon as I even just think about going outside to walk on the Earth and enjoy nature, her beauties and wonders, my heart is already filled with joy. The Earth gives me so much. I am so in love with her. It's a wonderful love—there is no betrayal. We entrust our heart to the Earth, and she entrusts herself to us, with her whole being.

Mother Earth is real. She is a living reality that you can touch, taste, smell, hear, and see. She has given us life. And when we die, we'll go back to her, and she'll bring us to life time and time again. There are people who have lost hope, who are tired of life on Earth, and who pray to be reborn elsewhere, in a heaven where there is no suffering. And yet they're not even sure whether such a place really exists. Astronomers have been able to look at many distant galaxies using powerful telescopes, but they haven't found anything as beautiful as this planet Earth. Where else would you want to go when Mother Earth is so beautiful, and always ready to embrace you and welcome you home?

I have learned that my home, my country, is the whole planet Earth. I do not limit my love to a tiny piece of land in Asia, Vietnam. I have experienced a lot of transformation and healing thanks to this insight. If your love is still too small, you have to enlarge your heart. Your love has to embrace the whole planet Earth.

Real change will only happen when we fall in love with our planet. Only love can show us how to live in harmony with nature and each other and save us from suffering the devastating effects of climate change. When we recognize the virtues and talents of the Earth, we feel connected to her, and love is born. We want to be connected. That is the meaning of love: to be at one. When you love someone, you want to take care of them as you would take care of yourself. When we love the Earth like this, it's a reciprocated love. We'll do anything for the benefit of the Earth, and the Earth will do anything for our well-being.

An Old Tree Produces New Blossoms

Biologically, I am getting older and older every day. But in some way, I am getting younger and younger. It's very strange. Every day I wake up and have new insight, like an old tree producing new flowers, and my love continues to grow.

In Vietnam there is a type of plum tree with yellow flowers, which can live a long time. Sometimes its trunk becomes twisted. At Lunar New Year, it produces a lot of lovely flowers that bloom not only on the small delicate branches, but even at the base of the trunk. I feel like that tree. In the morning I wake up, and there is a new insight springing up from deep down inside. It appears without effort. I don't have to practice hard at all. It's like when you plant a seed and water it, then it just grows.

If you come to my home in France in the month of April, you won't see any sunflowers. Yet the farmers have already planted the sunflower seeds. They've put manure and compost in the soil, and everything is ready. In early June, the stems will already have grown one or two feet tall, and within a month the sunflowers will be blooming everywhere. Our practice is to cultivate good seeds in the soil of our mind, knowing that they will mature and bloom in their own time. If we look deeply enough, we can already see the sunflowers in April.

Hide-and-Seek

Zen Patriarch Huyen Quang loved the chrysanthemum flower. He was the Third Master of the Bamboo Forest school in Vietnam, in the thirteenth and fourteenth centuries. He lived at Con Son Temple in the north of Vietnam, where he planted chrysanthemums in all the gardens around the temple.

When we love something, we are attached to its form and yet we know it's going to change and die, and this makes us suffer. A flower manifests; it buds, it blooms, it stays with us for a few weeks, and then it begins to change and its petals gradually start to wilt. At some point, the whole flower droops and dies. When we love a chrysanthemum, we have to see the chrysanthemum outside of birth, dwelling, changing, and death. When it manifests, we smile and we enjoy it. But when it is in hiding, we don't cry or feel sad. We say, "Next year I will see you again."

In my hermitage in France, there is a bush of japonica, Japanese quince. The bush usually blossoms in the spring, but one winter it had been quite warm and the flower buds had come early. During the night, a cold snap arrived and brought with it frost. The next day while doing walking meditation, I noticed that all the buds on the bush had died. When I noticed this I thought, "This New Year we will not have enough flowers to decorate the altar of the Buddha."

A few weeks later, the weather became warm again. As I walked in my garden, I saw new buds on the japonica manifesting another generation of flowers. I asked the japonica flowers: "Are you the same as the flowers that died in the frost, or are you different flowers?" The flowers replied, "We are not the same, and we are not different. When conditions are sufficient we manifest, and when conditions are not sufficient we go into hiding. It's as simple as that."

This is what the Buddha taught. When conditions are sufficient things manifest. When conditions are no longer sufficient things withdraw. They wait until the moment is right for them to manifest again.

Before giving birth to me, my mother was pregnant with another baby. She had a miscarriage, and that child wasn't born. When I was young I used to ask the question: Was that my brother or was that me? Who was trying to manifest at that time? If a baby is lost, it means that conditions were not sufficient for him to manifest and the child has decided to withdraw in order to wait for better conditions. "I had better withdraw; I'll come back again soon, my dearest." We have to respect his or her will. If you see the world with eyes like this, you will suffer much less. Was it my brother that my mother lost? Or maybe I was about to come out but instead I said, "It isn't time yet," so I withdrew.

At Home in the World

Greeting Each Other

Many years ago when I was visiting Taiwan, I was walking down a dirt road with some friends. A mother and her young son were walking toward us on the opposite side of the road, holding hands. Our eyes met and I greeted the young boy, placing my palms together, making a lotus bud with my hands in front of my heart in the traditional greeting, acknowledging the Buddha in him. With his mother still holding on to his hand, the boy smiled at me and, holding up his other hand in front of his chest, bowed and acknowledged the Buddha in me. Just after they passed, the little boy turned and looked back at us. His eyes widened, and it seemed to all of us as if he recognized me, and I felt we had met before. My friends and I stood watching as they walked away, out of sight.

I have on occasion thought of this sweet encounter as a lovely illustration of how we can all recognize the goodness and peace in each other. We are not strangers to each other. We are united by our Buddha nature. The desire to become an awakened person is strong in all of us. If we allow it to manifest, it will bring us—and many others—great happiness.

The Bell

When I was a young monk in Vietnam, each village temple had a big bell, similar to the bells in Christian churches in Europe. Whenever the bell was invited to sound, all the villagers would stop what they were doing and pause for a few moments to breathe in and out in mindfulness. At Plum Village, the community where I live in France, we do the same. Every time we hear the bell, whether it's our own activity bell or the bell from the nearby village church, we go back to ourselves and enjoy our breathing. When we breathe in, we say, silently, "Listen, listen," and when we breathe out, we say, "This wonderful sound brings me back to my true home."

Our true home is in the present moment. To live in the present moment is a miracle. The miracle is not to walk on water. The miracle is to walk on the green Earth in the present moment, to appreciate the peace and beauty that are available right now. Peace is all around us—in the world and in nature—and within us, in our bodies and our spirits. Once we learn to touch this peace, we will be healed and transformed. It is not a matter of faith; it is a matter of practice. We only need to find ways to bring our body and mind back to the present moment so we can touch what is refreshing, healing, and wondrous, within us and around us.

In Plum Village, our brothers and sisters program a bell of mindfulness on their computer. Every quarter of an hour, the bell sounds and they stop working or thinking, and they go back to their in-breath and out-breath; they come home to their body. They feel they are there, truly alive. They enjoy mindful breathing at least three times, and smile before they continue their work.

In our daily life we have to remind ourselves to come back to our body and take care of our body. Many of us have not been kind enough to our body. We have worked our body too hard; we have neglected it. When we spend two hours on our computer, we may entirely forget that we have a body. Our body is lonely; there is tension, there is pain. When the mind is not with the body, you are not really there, alive. We are truly alive only when our mind is with our body. And so when we hear the sound of the bell, it reminds us to go back to our body, to recognize the existence of our body, and to take care of our body. We enjoy breathing and bring our mind home to our body, and suddenly we are fully present in the here and now. We release the tension in our body and smile. This is an act of reconciliation, an act of love.

Our body is a wonder of life, just as everything surrounding us is a wonder of life—the gentle rain, the fresh air, a beautiful flower. Every one of us is a flower in the garden of humanity. We need to take care of our body so it can be a pleasant place for us to go home to.

Some years ago, I was taking a taxi in New York City, and I could tell that the driver was very unhappy. There was no peace or joy in him. He was not able to truly be alive while doing his job, and this was reflected in the way he was driving. Many of us are the same. We rush about, but we are not at one with what we are doing; we are not at peace. Our body is here, but our mind is somewhere else—in the past or the future, possessed by anger, frustration, hopes, or dreams. We are not really alive; we are not fully present; we are like ghosts. If our beautiful child were to come up to us and offer us a smile, would we be present to receive this wondrous gift? Or would we miss this precious opportunity to encounter life and each other? What a pity that would be.

The Soul of Ancient Europe

At noon in the Upper Hamlet of Plum Village, when we hear the
church bells of the surrounding villages, we are often practicing
walking meditation along the forest paths. I always stop to listen to
the bells together with the whole community as they resonate across
the valley.

A bell is always a bell; whether it's Catholic, Protestant,
Orthodox, or Buddhist, it is still a bell. Listening to the bell is a very
deep, very pleasant practice that brings peace, solidity, and freedom
to us every time we practice listening.

In the old days in Europe, people used to stop and say a prayer
every time they heard the church bells ringing. I hope that future
generations can preserve these bells across the landscape of Europe
and America, and that once more, whenever the bells sound, everyone will stop, and listen, and smile.

The first time I was deeply touched by church bells was while
visiting the ancient city of Prague. In the spring of 1992, we visited
Moscow and Leningrad. We offered a number of retreats and days
of mindfulness in Russia, before going on to countries in Eastern
Europe, and we also held a retreat in the city of Prague. After many
days of hard work, we were enjoying a free day, visiting the great city.
I was walking very slowly with a number of friends and monks and
nuns. We were looking at some postcards in front of a lovely little
church, in a narrow, very beautiful alley.

Suddenly the church bells started ringing. I don't know why, but
in that particular moment, the sound of the bells touched me deeply.
I had heard many church bells before, in France, in Switzerland,
and many other countries, but I had never heard bells like that. In
the sound of those bells, I felt that I was hearing the soul of ancient

Europe. I had been living in Europe for a long time, and I had seen a lot, but at that moment, the sound of the church bells brought me into deep connection with the soul of Europe.

Deep in the background of the Prague church bells, I could hear the bell of a Buddhist temple in my store consciousness. It was a kind of encounter between one civilization and another. When you get in touch deeply with one, you have a chance to get in touch deeply with the other. So those of you who have Christian or Jewish roots should try to keep your roots. The more you are rooted in your own tradition, the better you will understand Buddhism. It has been like that for me. The more I got in touch with Christianity and Judaism, the better I could understand Buddhism.

Anything good needs time to ripen. When enough conditions come together, what has been latent in us for a long time can arise. When I first came to Europe, I was preoccupied with the work of trying to put an end to the killing in Vietnam. I was traveling a lot, talking to many people, and holding press conferences. I was so busy that I did not have enough time to truly encounter the soul of Europe. Prague hadn't been destroyed during the Second World War. It was a beautiful city that was still intact, which is perhaps why the sound of the church bells touched me so.

When you practice in one spiritual tradition, it can help you understand other traditions better. It is like a tree with roots. When transplanted, it is able to absorb nutrients from the new soil, the new environment. In Prague we stood there very quietly and listened to the bells.

When you hear the sound of a bell, you may not feel anything at first. You may think the sound of the bell has nothing much to do with you, but any bell can speak to you. Any bell is an invitation.

A Marketplace Dream

One autumn while I was teaching in England, I had a dream that
stayed with me long after. My brother and I were at an open market
when a man led us to a stall in one corner of the market. When we
arrived there, I immediately recognized that every item on display
represented an event that I had directly lived and experienced with
my brother and others who were close to me. Almost all the items,
the experiences, were of suffering—poverty, fire, floods, storms,
hunger, racial discrimination, ignorance, hatred, fear, despair, political
oppression, injustice, war, death, and misery. As I touched each item,
a feeling of sorrow arose in me and, at the same time, a feeling of
compassion.

At the center of the stall stood a long table, on which were dis-
played a number of elementary school notebooks. I recognized one
notebook was mine and another was my brother's. Looking through
the pages of my notebook, I recognized many significant, happy
experiences from my childhood as well as many experiences of
suffering. My brother's notebook recorded our experiences together
as little boys. At the time I had the dream, I was writing the memoirs
of my childhood, but I had not included any of the materials that
were in those notebooks. Perhaps they were experiences that I had
lived only in my dreams and had forgotten when I woke up. Perhaps
they were experiences from previous lives. I was not sure which, but
I was certain that these experiences were authentically mine, and
I thought about bringing these materials home so I could include
them in my memoirs. I was very pleased with this idea, as I didn't
want to forget again.

Just as I was thinking this, the man who had invited us to look
at his stall said something terrible. Standing at my side he said,

"You will have to go through all of this again!" He spoke with such authority, as though he were a judge issuing a solemn verdict, and I was condemned to suffer. He sounded like God, or Destiny. I was shocked. Do I really have to go through all that suffering again, all those storms and floods, those fires of hunger, racial discrimination, ignorance, hatred, despair, fear, sorrow, political oppression, misery, war, and death? I had the feeling I had suffered these things for countless lifetimes already with my brother and my companions from the past. For so long, we could not see the light at the end of the tunnel, and now finally we were in a place with space and freedom. Would we really have to go through all of those experiences again?

At first I felt a kind of revulsion, thinking, "Oh no!" but in a split second, my reaction changed. I pointed two fingers of my right hand directly into the man's face and told him with all my determination and might, "You cannot frighten me. Even if I have to go through all of this again, I'll do it! Not just once, but thousands more times if necessary. And all of us will do it together!"

At that moment I woke up, and at first I could not remember the contents of the dream. I only knew I had just had a very powerful and important dream. So I stayed in bed and practiced conscious breathing, and slowly the details came back. I had a feeling that the man represented something; and that he was telling me something I needed to hear. At first I thought that I was going to die very soon and begin my destined journey again. But I felt calm. Dying was not a problem. I was not afraid. All I needed to do was to tell Sister True Emptiness, one of my closest companions over the past thirty years, so that she and others would be prepared. But soon I realized that I didn't have to die yet. The dream had to have a deeper meaning.

I looked at the clock. It was 3:30 in the morning. I thought about all the children in Vietnam, Cambodia, Somalia, Yugoslavia, and South America, and other places where there is so much suffering, and I felt a strong sense of solidarity with all of them. I felt ready to undergo these hardships with them, again and again.

You, my brothers and sisters, are my companions. You are truly bodhisattvas, riding on the waves of birth and death, without drowning in birth and death. We have gone though interminable suffering, endless tunnels of sorrow and darkness. But we have practiced, and through the practice, we have obtained some insight and freedom. Now it is time for us to join together and bring our strength to bear on the challenges that lie before us. I am sure we will do better this time.

Footsteps of the Buddha

In 1968, on my way to Paris to help set up the Buddhist delegation at the peace talks, I stopped in India, hoping to have an opportunity to visit the place where the Buddha reached enlightenment. From New Delhi I took a plane to go to Patna, north of the Ganges River. From Patna I could go to Bodhgaya where the Buddha was enlightened. That plane followed the footsteps of the Buddha along the Ganges River.

The Buddha didn't travel by car, by airplane, or by train. He just walked. He walked to many cities. Once he even walked as far as Delhi. He visited over fifteen kingdoms on foot. Knowing that, as I was looking down on the Ganges, I could see his footsteps everywhere. The Buddha's footsteps continue to bring his solidity, freedom, peace, joy, and happiness everywhere.

It was very nice to have fifteen minutes to visualize the Buddha down there, walking and sharing his happiness, his enlightenment, his peace, and his joy with the Earth and with the human beings who inhabited that region of the Earth. I was moved to tears, looking down as I sat on the plane, seeing the presence of the Buddha in the here and now. Looking down, I vowed that I would practice walking meditation in order to bring the steps of the Buddha to other parts of the world. We can walk in Europe, in the Americas, in Australia, in Africa, and we can continue the Buddha, bringing peace and joy, solidity, and freedom to many parts of the world.

I have been all over the world. I have shared the practice of walking meditation with so many people. I have many friends, both monastic and lay, who have been walking like that on all five continents. So the Buddha is now everywhere, and not just in the delta of the Ganges River.

Visiting India that time, I had an opportunity to climb the Gridhrakuta Mountain. The Buddha used to like staying there, in the vicinity of Rajagriha, the capital of Magadha, the country where King Bimbisara reigned.

A group of friends—monks, nuns, and laypeople—climbed the Gridhrakuta Mountain with me. There was a monk with us whose name was Mahagosananda. He was still young at the time. Later on he became the patriarch of Cambodia. We climbed the Gridhrakuta Mountain slowly and mindfully. When we arrived at the top, close to the place where the Buddha used to sit, we all sat down and we were able to see the same beautiful sunset that the Buddha used to see. We sat and we practiced mindful breathing and contemplated the beauty of the sunset. We were using the eyes of the Buddha to admire and enjoy the beautiful sunset.

King Bimbisara had a stone path built from the foot of the mountain to the top so that the Buddha could climb up and down more easily. That stone path is still there. If you go there, you can also enjoy climbing the mountain, using the same stone path, and you may visualize that the Buddha has stepped on those very same stones.

Two Minutes of Peace

When I was in India in 1997, I had the opportunity to meet with the vice president of India and president of the Parliament, Mr. K. R. Narayanan. Our discussion took place on the opening day of the budget session of the parliament, just before three new members of the government were to be sworn into office. I thanked Mr. Narayanan for taking the time to meet with me on such a busy day. He replied that, busy or not, it was always important for him to meet with a spiritual person. We sat together and discussed how the members of parliament could apply the practice of mindfulness, deep listening, and loving speech in their sessions.

I suggested that it would be good to begin every session with the practice of mindful breathing. A few lines of text could be read out to bring awareness into everyone's mind, such as: "Dear colleagues, the people who have elected us expect us to communicate with each other using kind, respectful speech and to listen deeply to each other before sharing our insights so that the parliament can make the best decisions for the benefit of the nation and the people." It would take less than one minute to read. I suggested that anytime things got too heated during a debate or if representatives started to insult or condemn each other, then someone would have the right to invite a bell and request everyone to stop arguing and be silent for one or two minutes. In that moment, all the representatives could practice mindful breathing to calm themselves down.

When we say, "Let us observe two minutes of silence," people usually don't know what to do during the two minutes. But those of us who practice mindfulness know exactly what to do; we know how to breathe, how to focus our attention on our breathing, and how to relax the body and mind and allow compassion to be born. A moment of silence does not cost anything. It does not need a budget. A moment of silence can restore peace, understanding, and insight. Anyone can do it. You don't need to be a Buddhist.

Mr. Narayanan was very attentive to what I said and invited me to come back and address the Indian Parliament on that issue. Ten days later, I was leading a retreat in Madras, and someone showed me a newspaper article reporting that they had set up a Committee on Ethics, which had the task of improving the quality of communication in the parliament.

This kind of practice of nonviolence is possible everywhere, in every country. We urgently need to reduce the animosity and tension in the government. We are not helpless. We have to do our best; we have to stop the war inside ourselves. This is the practice of peace, and it can be done in every moment. If we do not practice peace in our lives, war will continue to break out within us and in the world around us.

Drops of Compassion

I was in California on September 11, 2001, when we heard the news of the destruction of the Twin Towers in New York. The energy of anger and fear around was tremendous. When a whole nation is experiencing such strong anger and fear like that, it wouldn't take much to do something destructive. It is easy to start a war in such moments. We need to have clarity of mind in order to know what to do and what not to do, in order to avoid making the situation worse.

I was scheduled to give a public talk three days later to four thousand people in Berkeley. We were a delegation of eighty monks and nuns, and we wore our saffron *sanghati* robes for the talk. The emotion was palpable. It was a national emotion. We knew that we needed to be able to balance the collective energy of anger, fear, and discrimination with the collective energy of mindfulness, compassion, and brotherhood. It is very important to counterbalance fear with calm and peace.

We began with a session of calming: we offered a guided meditation and some chanting to help everyone practice mindfulness of breathing to calm the body and mind and to embrace the fear that was present. I offered a prayer for healing and peace, to touch our deep aspiration to offer humanity the best flowers and fruits of our practice: lucidity, solidity, brotherhood, understanding, and compassion. I reminded everyone that responding to hatred with hatred will only cause hatred to multiply a thousandfold, and that only with compassion can we transform hatred and anger. I invited them to go home to themselves and practice mindful breathing and mindful walking, to calm down their strong emotions and to allow lucidity to prevail. Only when we understand, can compassion arise. When the drop of compassion begins to form in our hearts and minds, we can begin to develop concrete responses to a situation.

Our individual consciousness reflects the collective consciousness. Each of us can begin right now to practice calming our anger, looking deeply at the roots of the hatred and violence in our society and in our world. Each of us can practice listening deeply with compassion in order to hear and understand what we have not yet heard and understood. When we have listened and looked deeply, we may begin to develop the energy of brotherhood and sisterhood between all nations, which is the deepest spiritual heritage of all religious and cultural traditions. In this way, peace and understanding within the whole world is increased day by day. Developing the nectar of compassion in our own heart is the only effective spiritual response to hatred and violence.

The Times of India

On another visit to India in 2008, I was invited by the *Times of India* to be guest editor for the day. It was the commemoration day for Mahatma Gandhi, and the newspaper thought it appropriate to invite a Buddhist monk to be guest editor for a special edition on the theme of peace. I accepted the invitation and was accompanied by many monastic brothers and sisters. As soon as we arrived at the newsroom in the morning, some very bad news came in. A terrorist attack, a bombing, had just taken place in Mumbai, and many people had been killed. The atmosphere was very tense, and I was asked to join a meeting of all the editors. I remember us all sitting there in silence around a huge table.

One of the editors looked up and asked, "What should we do when we receive such terrible news on a day like today?" It was very hard to answer. I practiced mindful breathing for a while and then I said, "Dear friends, we have to report it. But we have to report it in such a way that can promote understanding and compassion, and not give rise to more anger and despair. And that depends on you, and on the way you report the incident."

When a tragic incident like this occurs, we have to look deeply and ask ourselves the question, "What has driven the terrorists to do such a thing? What kinds of views and perceptions must have been accumulating in them to drive them to do such a terrible thing to their own countrymen?" They must have a lot of anger and hate and a lot of wrong perceptions. They may feel wronged, mistreated, or misunderstood. They may believe they are acting in the name of justice, or in the name of God. We have to look deeply in order to understand acts of violence like this and the motivation behind them.

And when we have gained some insight, then the news we report will embody our understanding and compassion.

There are many ways of reporting. Much of the news that we consume in newspapers, on the radio, television, or the Internet contains a lot of violence, fear, hatred, discrimination, and despair. We can say that a lot of news is toxic; it is poisoning our hearts and minds, and the hearts and minds of our children. As journalists, we need to report events truthfully, while at the same time watering the seed of understanding and compassion in our readers and viewers. And as consumers, we need to use our mindfulness to be aware of our thoughts, feelings, and perceptions when we consume the news, so that we can protect ourselves. We need to know how much is enough. Mindfulness helps us protect the sovereignty of our hearts and minds and prevent negative seeds from being watered in our consciousness.

Our way of communicating with one another, of speaking and listening, is very important. Each of us can make the commitment to not water the seeds of violence, hate, discrimination, and despair in ourselves and in our relationships. Equally importantly, we can commit to actively watering the seeds of understanding, tolerance, and nondiscrimination within ourselves and our society.

A Relaxing Bus Ride

One day I was sitting on a bus in India with a friend who was organizing my visit there. My friend belonged to the caste that has been discriminated against for thousands of years. I was enjoying the view out
the window, when I noticed that he was quite tense. I knew he was
worried about making sure my time was enjoyable, so I said, "Please
relax. I am enjoying my visit very much. Everything is going very well."
There was really no need for him to worry. He sat back and smiled,
but after just a few moments, he was tense again. When I looked at
him, I could see the struggle that had been going on for four or five
thousand years, within him as a person, and within his entire caste.
Now, organizing my visit, he continued to struggle. He could relax for
one second, and then he would begin to tense up again.

We all have this tendency to struggle in our bodies and our minds.
We believe that happiness is possible only in the future. That is why
the practice of realizing "I have arrived" in the present moment,
of dwelling happily in the present moment, is very important. The
realization that we have already arrived, that we don't have to travel
any further, that we are already home, can bring us peace and joy. We
already have more than enough conditions to be happy. We only need
to allow ourselves to arrive fully in the present moment, and we will
be able to touch them.

Sitting on the bus, my friend couldn't allow himself to dwell
peacefully in the present moment. He was still worrying about how
to make me comfortable even though I was already comfortable. So
I suggested that he allow himself to just be, but it was not easy for
him, because the habit energy of anxiety had been there for such a
long time. Even after our bus had arrived at the station and we had
gotten off, my friend still could not enjoy himself. My entire visit to

India went very well, and the way he organized everything had been excellent, yet I am afraid that to this day, he is still unable to relax. We are under the influence of previous generations of our ancestors and our society. The practice of stopping and looking deeply is to stop our habit energy being sustained by the negative seeds that have been transmitted to us. When we are able to stop, we do it for all our ancestors, and we end the vicious circle that is called samsara.

We have to live in such a way that liberates our ancestors and future generations inside us. Joy, peace, freedom, and harmony are not individual matters. If we do not liberate our ancestors, we will be in bondage all our lives, and we will transmit our negative habit energies to our children and grandchildren. Now is the time to liberate ourselves and to liberate them. It is the same thing. This is the teaching of interbeing. As long as our ancestors in us are still suffering, we ourselves cannot be at peace. If we take one step mindfully, happily, touching the Earth in freedom, we do it for all our previous and future generations. They all arrive with us at the same moment, and all of us find peace and happiness at the same time.

Olive Trees

One year I went to Italy for a retreat, and I noticed that the olive trees were growing in small groups. I was surprised and asked: "Why do you plant olive trees in groups of three or four?"

Our Italian friends explained that each group of three or four is actually just one tree. Some years earlier, it had been so cold that all the olive trees had died. But deep down at the level of the roots they were still alive. After the harsh winter, when spring came, the young shoots sprouted. So instead of having one trunk, the olive trees had three or four trunks. On the surface, it appeared that there were three or four olive trees, but in fact they were one.

If you are siblings of the same parents, you are part of the same tree. You have the same roots, the same father and mother. These three or four olive trees also have the same block of roots. They look like different trees, but they are just one. It would be odd if one tree discriminated against the other, if they were to fight and kill each other; that would be sheer ignorance. Looking deeply, they know that they are brothers and sisters; they are truly one.

Walking Freely

I remember one beautiful walking meditation that we led in Italy, in the center of Rome, in 2010. There were about 1,500 people, and about a dozen children were walking beside me at the front holding both my hands. The city had closed all the roads for us, and about twenty meters ahead of us, eight big police officers were walking together. What was unusual was that they were also walking with a lot of ease, very freely, stopping and guiding the traffic and pedestrians with kindness and smiles. It seemed as though these eight officers were also taking part in the walking meditation; as though the police officers and the people were one.

There has perhaps never been so much freedom in the capital's streets. We left footprints of freedom with every step. There was no stress, and the city center came to a halt for the pleasure of enjoying walking. In front of the eight police officers, a police vehicle was driving at the same speed as the walking meditation. All the people walking along the streets, standing in the public squares, or looking out from buildings along our route were able to witness the freedom we felt. Even though we were a large crowd, the walking meditation was nothing like a protest. There were no flags, no whistles, no drums, no banners, and no shouts. No one was asking anything of anyone else; there was no energy of struggle or resistance, and there were no demands being made. Everything took place in total silence and everyone was smiling. Everyone was following their breathing and enjoying their footsteps in the city. Peace and joy, sisterhood and brotherhood were truly present, clear for all to see.

We had begun the walk at the Piazza San Marco, where I offered some guidance to everyone on the practice of walking meditation before setting off. Within fifteen minutes, over a thousand had gathered. We all walked mindfully and peacefully in silence along the roads in the ancient city center and finally arrived at the Piazza Navona to practice sitting meditation in the square. As we entered the piazza, someone was playing the saxophone, but as soon as they saw us they stopped. The whole piazza became a silent open-air meditation hall. It was a beautiful sunny day. I offered a guided meditation for the whole crowd to practice looking deeply into their true nature, into their ancestors, their parents, and into life and nonself, right in the heart of Italy's capital. It was very beautiful, nourishing, and healing for all.

We have practiced walking and sitting meditation in many countries, bringing footsteps of peace to major cities around the world. We have held peace walks in Paris, New York, and Los Angeles. One thousand people walked in meditation along the banks of Hanoi's famous Hoan Kiem Lake in 2008, and four thousand of us sat peacefully in meditation in London's Trafalgar Square in 2012. Wherever we walk in meditation, we generate a powerful collective energy of compassion, forgiveness, and peace.

I Have Arrived

A Classroom Dream

One night over twenty-five years ago, I dreamed that I was a student in college. Although I was already over sixty at the time, in the dream I was only twenty-one. In the dream, it was announced that I had been accepted into a class taught by a very distinguished professor, the most beloved professor in the university. It was a very prestigious class and the most difficult for a student to get into.

I was so happy to be accepted and went straight to the office to inquire where the class would be held. I saw many students streaming in, and then suddenly I saw a young person my age who looked just like me. His face, the color of his clothing, and everything looked exactly like me. I was very surprised. Was that me or was that not me? Was he another me outside of me? He was trying to find his way. I was very curious and asked the lady in the office whether that young man had been accepted into the same class. She said, "No, absolutely not. You have been accepted but not him."

I was told that the class would be held on the top floor of the building that very morning. I started to make my way to the class, and halfway up the stairs I asked some others, "What is the subject of this class?" "Music," they answered. I thought it strange that I should be accepted into a music class taught by a distinguished music professor, as I was not a music student at all. I was a little concerned, but figured that since I had been accepted into the class, there must be a good reason, so I needn't worry.

When I came to the door of the classroom, I opened it and looked inside. I had imagined there would be only twenty-five or thirty students in the class, but to my great suprise, I saw more than a thousand. It was a real assembly. Looking out through the windows, I saw an incredibly beautiful landscape. I saw the moon, the sun, constellations of stars, and snow-capped mountain peaks. It was inexpressibly beautiful. I cannot describe the feeling I had to stand there and take in this incredible scene. It was such an honor to be in that class.

Suddenly I was told that I would have to give a presentation when the professor arrived. I was at a complete loss. I didn't know anything about music, and yet I was expected to give a presentation on music! What's more, I was to be the first one to give a presentation. I looked around me and instinctively searched my pockets. I felt something hard in my pocket and I took it out; it was a small bell. I realized, "This is an instrument of music. I can present it." Because I had been practicing with the bell for so many years already, I regained my confidence.

I got ready to speak, and just as they were announcing the professor's arrival, I woke up. I regretted waking up so much. If only the dream had continued for another two or three minutes, I would have been able to see the beloved professor that everyone adored.

After I woke up, I tried to remember all the details of the dream and decipher it. It seemed that the young man who hadn't been accepted into the class was also me. Perhaps he was an earlier me, still caught in certain kinds of views and not yet free enough to be accepted into a master class. But I had grown and left him behind. I had attained some kind of insight that enabled me to free myself of attachment to views, or whatever else it was that was still holding the young man back.

Each of us may have views that we hold on to and consider to be the truth, and we are attached to those views. But if you get caught in your views, then you have no chance to progress. My dream was a reminder that sometimes I have to leave part of myself behind in order to be able to advance on my path.

Lettuce

When you plant lettuce, you don't blame the lettuce if it does not grow well. You look into the reasons why it is not doing well. It may need fertilizer, or more water, or less sun. You never blame the lettuce. Yet if we have problems with our friends or our family, we blame the other person. But if we know how to take care of others, they will grow well, just like the lettuce. Blaming has no positive effect at all, nor does trying to persuade by means of reason or argument. That is my experience. No blame, no reasoning, no argument—just understanding. If you understand, and you show that you understand, you can love, and any difficult situation will improve.

One day in Paris, I gave a lecture about not blaming the lettuce. After the talk, I was doing walking meditation by myself, and when I turned the corner of a building, I overheard an eight-year-old girl telling her mother, "Mommy, remember to water me. I am your lettuce." I was so pleased that she had understood my point completely. Then I heard her mother reply, "Yes, darling, and I am your lettuce as well. So please don't forget to water me too." Mother and daughter practicing together; it was so beautiful.

Our Two Hands

One day I was trying to hang a picture on the wall. My left hand was holding a nail and my right hand a hammer. That day I was not very mindful and instead of pounding on the nail, I pounded on my finger. When I hit my finger, the left hand suffered. Right away the right hand put down the hammer and immediately started to take care of the left hand with gentleness and compassion, as though she were taking care of herself. She didn't see it as her duty. It was very natural—my right hand does things for my left hand as if she were doing them for herself.

My right hand considers the suffering of my left hand as her own suffering. That is why she did everything to take care of the left hand. My left hand was not angry at all. My left hand did not say, "You, right hand, you have done me wrong. Give me that hammer. I want justice!"

The left hand had no such thinking. There's an inherent wisdom in my left hand, the wisdom of nondiscrimination. When we have this kind of wisdom, we don't suffer. My left hand never fights my right hand. Both hands enjoy harmony and understanding. When one hand suffers, they both suffer; when one hand is happy, they are both happy.

Look into Your Hand

I have a Vietnamese friend, an artist, who has been away from his homeland for nearly forty years. He hasn't seen his mother in all that time. When he misses his mother, all he has to do is look at his hands and he feels better. His mother, a traditional Vietnamese woman, could only read a few characters and had never studied Western philosophy or science. Yet before he left Vietnam, she held his hand, and told him, "Whenever you miss me, look into your hand, my child. You will see me immediately." For nearly forty years now, he has done just that and and has looked into his hand many times.

The presence of his mother is not just genetic. Her spirit, her hopes, and her life are also present in him. Looking at his hand, he can penetrate deeply into the reality of beginningless and endless time. He can see that thousands of generations before him and thousands of generations after him are all him. From time immemorial until the present moment, his life has never been interrupted, and his hand is still there, a beginningless and endless reality.

Sometimes when I practice calligraphy, I invite my mother, my father, or my teacher to draw the circle with me. Drawing the circle together, I touch the insight of no self, and it becomes a deep practice of meditation. The meditation, work, joy, and life become one.

We can find the presence of our father, our mother, and our ancestors in every cell of our body. Not only meditation but science also tells us this. Our parents are not only outside of us. Whenever we are able to breathe mindfully and calm our body and mind, our parents in us are breathing mindfully and calming themselves at the same time. If we are able to generate a feeling of joy and compassion, our parents in us also experience that joy and compassion.

Our parents may never have been fortunate enough to practice mindfulness and transform their suffering. Looking at them with the eyes of compassion, we can share with them our own joy, peace, and forgiveness.

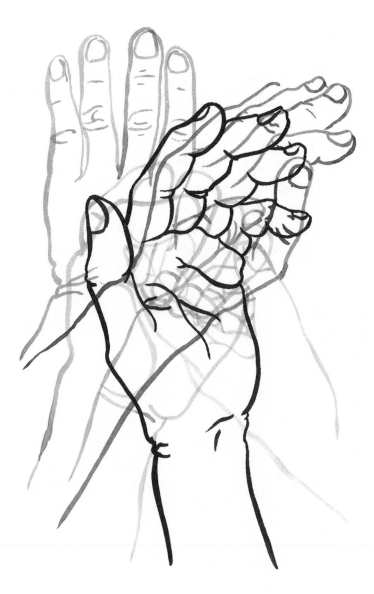

Give Me Some Tobacco!

In recent years, prisons have had access to books on meditation, magazines, and even recordings of mindfulness talks. I often receive letters from prisoners, usually from prisons in North America. One inmate wrote to me, saying, "When I stand at the top of the staircase and look down, I see other inmates running up and down, and I can see their suffering, their agitation. I wish they could do what I do, and walk up and down the staircase in mindfulness, following their breathing. When I do that, I feel peace within myself, and when I feel peace within myself, I can see very clearly the suffering of the other inmates."

Another time I heard from a prisoner on death row who had received two copies of one of my books, *Being Peace*. He himself had enjoyed the book and had started practicing sitting meditation in his cell. One day the fellow in the cell next to his banged on the wall and shouted out, asking for tobacco.

Although the prisoner who meditated didn't smoke anymore, he still had some tobacco. He took the first page of *Being Peace*, wrapped some tobacco in it, and sneaked it to the other side with the hope that the other person might enjoy reading *Being Peace*. He just gave a small amount of the tobacco he had, and the next time his neighbor asked for tobacco, he used page two, then page three. Finally he had transferred the whole book, page by page, to the other prisoner.

In the beginning his neighbor had banged and shouted and cursed. But soon he became much quieter. Eventually he became very calm. On the day his neighbor was released, as he passed in front of his cell, they looked at each other, and together recited a sentence from the book, which they both knew by heart.

It is clear that punishment is not the only solution to crime. There are much more effective and compassionate things we can do to help those who have broken the law. I was once asked to write a letter of encouragement to a prisoner named Daniel, who was on death row in Jackson, Georgia, in the United States. He was nineteen when he committed his crime, and had spent thirteen years—his entire adulthood—behind bars. He had read a book of mine and found it very helpful as the time of his execution was drawing near.

I sent Daniel a short handwritten note that said, in part: "Many people around you have a lot of anger, hate, and despair, which prevents them from getting in touch with the fresh air, the blue sky, or the fragrant rose. They are in a kind of prison. But if you practice compassion, if you can see the suffering in the people around you, and if every day you try to do something to help them suffer less, then you are free. One day with compassion is worth more than one hundred days without it."

We who suffer less on the outside can do something to help those on the inside. The death penalty merely reveals our weakness and helplessness. We don't know what to do and we give up. It is a cry of despair when a society has to kill people. It is possible to reconcile justice and compassion, and to demonstrate that true justice must contain both compassion and understanding.

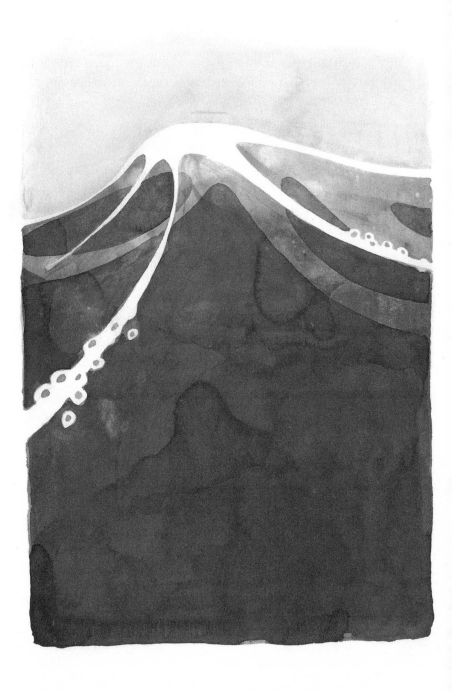

The Wave and the Water

A friend of mine who was a research scientist went through a tremendous spiritual crisis one winter. Hearing of this, I sent him a drawing of a wave riding on silky-smooth water. Beneath the drawing I wrote, "As always, the wave lives the life of a wave and, at the same time, the life of water. When you breathe, you breathe for all of us." As I wrote those words, I felt that I was swimming alongside him, helping him to get through that time of great difficulty; and fortunately, it helped us both.

Most people view themselves as waves and forget that they are also water. They are used to living in the realm of birth and death, and they forget about the realm of no birth and no death. Just as a wave lives the life of water, so, too, do we live the life of no birth and no death. We need to know this, and to be in touch with the reality that we are living the life of no birth and no death. The word *know* here is very important. To know is to realize. Realization is mindfulness. All the work of meditation is aimed at awakening us in order to know one thing: that birth and death can never touch us in any way whatsoever.

The Googleplex

In 2013 I led a day of mindfulness practice for Google employees at the Google headquarters in California—they call it the "Googleplex." There were about thirty monks and nuns in our delegation, and over seven hundred Google employees had signed up for the day. Starting early in the morning, we led sessions of sitting meditation, walking meditation, eating in mindfulness, and total relaxation—exactly like a day of mindfulness in Plum Village.

The Google employees were young, intelligent, and creative, and we could see they invested themselves wholeheartedly into the practice. The energy of concentration and presence was very strong, and they practiced very well. I think the reason they practiced so wholeheartedly is because they suffer. They were thirsty for a kind of spiritual practice that could help them suffer less. We knew that they had been working very hard. All companies are striving for success, and there's a strong desire to be "number one." That is why many young people invest all their time and energy into their work, into their company, and they don't have time to take care of their body, their feelings, their emotions, and their relationships. Even if they do have time, they may not know what to do with that time in order to really take care of their body and mind.

I shared with everyone how to practice walking meditation, and we began the day by walking slowly, mindfully, in silence around the campus. After fifteen minutes or so, we sat down quietly, without saying a word. I held my cup of tea in my two hands and was enjoying my tea as people began to arrive, to sit down all together, and to follow their breathing. We sat there peacefully for a long time, enjoying the silence and stillness of the morning. Meanwhile, many employees were arriving late for work, and each time someone came around the corner, they stopped suddenly in surprise. They saw something happening: a lot of people sitting down and doing nothing, just breathing. It was so quiet! It was something entirely new and unexpected. Time is no longer money. Time is peace; time is life.

Many of us are so busy and work so much that we don't have time to live. Our work can take up all our life. We may even be addicted to our work, not because we need the money, but because we don't know how to handle the suffering and loneliness inside, and so we take refuge in our work. There are times we don't know what to do with our loneliness, pain, and despair inside. We try to look for something to cover it up. We check email, we pick up a newspaper, we listen to the news, anything to forget the loneliness and suffering inside. Our body is restless, our mind is restless, and we don't know what to do. We try to sit, but it's as though we're sitting on burning coals. We may take a walk, but it's as though we're walking on fire.

When the energy of restlessness manifests itself, we have to recognize what is going on and say, "Hello my restlessness. I know you are there. I will take good care of you." Then we start to practice mindful breathing, and bring our mind home to our body. When mind and body are together and you are established in the here and now, then you can get in touch with life and take care of the feelings inside. Then nature reveals itself and all its wonders. If we keep working so hard, we will not have enough time to live; we will not have enough time to touch life's wonders and get the nourishment and the healing we need. We need this insight in order to free ourselves from our restlessness. In the country of the present moment, we can heal ourselves and enjoy life deeply.

Is the Buddha in the Car?

In Vietnam, as well as in other Buddhist countries, people often have a Buddha statue in their car, truck or bus to protect them from accident and injury.

One day, while riding on a bus I asked my attendant, "Do you think the Buddha is in this bus with us or not?" He replied, "Yes, I think he is." I said, "Are you sure?'

It is easy to tell whether the Buddha is on the bus or not. If there are fifty people on the bus and there is just one person breathing in mindfulness then we can say the Buddha is on the bus. If not just one, but two, three, or even five people are breathing mindfully, calmly enjoying the view, then we can be sure that the Buddha is really present, and not just his statue.

Driving in the car, we only need one person in the car breathing mindfully to know the Buddha is present with us. With the presence of the Buddha, the bus or car is transformed into a place of meditation and awareness. With the Buddha in the car, everyone is safer and protected by his energy of mindfulness.

The presence of the Buddha, the energy of awakening, can accompany us in every moment of our lives. Before starting the car, we can ask ourselves, "Is the Buddha in the car?" If we are able to breathe in mindfulness, then the presence of the Buddha will be felt right away, and his energy will protect us as we drive. The Buddha's presence in the car makes every moment of the journey a moment worth living. The more of us who are breathing mindfully, the stronger the presence of the Buddha will be. And yet we often forget that with our mindful breathing we have this great power: to make the Buddha manifest right there in the car.

On one of our pilgrimages to India, it took eleven buses to transport our delegation of over three hundred practitioners and in each bus there was a statue of the Buddha. But having a Buddha statue—whether it's made of simple plastic or precious jade—doesn't guarantee that the Buddha is in the car. The only thing that assures the presence of the Buddha in the car is when at least one person is breathing mindfully.

I, myself, was practicing mindful breathing, but I wanted to be sure that the Buddha would be sitting on each bus, not just in my bus. So I suggested that each bus should have a bell, and that from time to time the bell would be invited to remind everyone to breathe mindfully. If everyone is breathing mindfully, then we can be sure that the Buddha is on the bus.

Wherever we are, every car should have a bell that we can invite to sound, to remind ourselves to come back to our mindful breathing and to the present moment. This is what will truly protect us. Not a statue of the Buddha, but our own mindfulness.

Walking on Country Paths

I like to walk along country paths lined with wild grasses lining the path. I place each foot on the earth in mindfulness, knowing that I am walking on the wondrous Earth. In such moments, existence becomes a miraculous and mysterious reality. People usually consider walking on water or in thin air to be a miracle. But I think the real miracle is not to walk either on water or in thin air, but to walk on the Earth. Every day we are engaged in a miracle that we don't even recognize: the blue sky, the white clouds, the green leaves, and the curious eyes of a child. All is a miracle.

When we walk, we're not walking alone. Our parents and ancestors are walking with us. They're present in every cell of our bodies. So each step that brings us healing and happiness also brings healing and happiness to our parents and ancestors. Every mindful step has the power to transform us and all our ancestors within us, including our animal, plant, and mineral ancestors. We don't walk for ourselves alone. When we walk, we walk for our family and for the whole world.

One Step

One day on a teaching tour in China, our delegation from Plum Village had an opportunity to climb the sacred Wutai Shan Mountain. Our tourist guide had led many groups, perhaps even hundreds of groups, up the mountain. But on that day we proposed that instead of leading, she would follow us, because we had our own way of walking.

At the foot of the mountain, I gave instructions as to how to walk. Breathing in, we make one step; breathing out, we make another step. Because there are thousands of steps, and we want to enjoy every step, our aim is not to get to the top of the mountain. Our aim is to touch peace and joy with every step. We had to walk on the right side of the steps as we climbed. Many groups overtook us. They would turn around and glare at us, trying to see who it was that was moving at a snail's pace up the mountain. It was not easy for our guide. I remember the walk very clearly. I would breathe in and put my left foot on the step, and then, breathe out and bring my right foot up. We were able to do it in such a way that pleasure and joy were possible with every step. We stopped every ten steps, to have a look down and enjoy the view and continue to breathe. Then we would continue. When we arrived at the top of the mountain, we were not tired at all.

In our delegation, there was a nun who could speak Chinese, and on the bus she overheard the tourist guide telling her col-league, "This monk is amazing. I have led hundreds of groups up the mountain, and I always arrive exhausted. But today for the first time, I arrived feeling refreshed. He really is incredible." At that time in China, the tourist guides had to submit reports on visitors' activities to the police. She went on to say, "I have finished my report on what they did and what the monk said today. But I haven't submitted it yet, because what he said was so interesting I want to read my notes again."

So whether you are walking at the railway station, at the airport, or along the bank of a river, make sure that every step you make brings you joy, relaxation, and happiness. Every step can be healing, whether you are walking with others or walking alone. We should not miss a single step. With every step, we arrive into our life. Every step helps us to stop running—running not only in the body, but running in the mind. Running has become a habit and we're not capable of enjoying our life in the here and now. Even in our sleep, in our dreams, we continue to run. So to truly arrive and stop with every step is a training. We need to train how to stop.

Every time you walk even a short distance, whether it's from your home to the bus stop, or from the parking lot to your workplace, you can choose to walk in such a way that every step can bring you joy, peace, and happiness. You may like to remember that others are also walking like that, and we can feel connected with each other. Connection is very important. It is not because you have a telephone that you can feel connected. I have never had a cell phone, and yet I have never felt disconnected from anyone. What connects us is our mindful walking, our mindful steps. So if you want to connect with others, all you need to do is to practice walking meditation every morning after breakfast on your way to work. Walking like that, in peace and freedom, we become connected right away.

Belonging

When I was a child, families were bigger. Parents, cousins, uncles, aunts, grandparents, and children all lived together. The houses were surrounded by trees where the family would hang hammocks and organize picnics. People did not have the kinds of problems we have today. When their mother and father argued, the children could always escape by running to an aunt or an uncle. They had other people besides their parents to take refuge in.

The nuclear family, consisting of two parents and a few children, is a relatively recent invention. Sometimes in such a small family, there is not enough air to breathe. When there is trouble between the parents, the whole family is affected. The atmosphere in the house is heavy, and there is nowhere to escape to.

Sometimes a child may go into the bathroom and lock the door just to be alone, but there is still no escape; the heavy atmosphere permeates the bathroom, too. So the child grows up with many seeds of suffering then later transmits these seeds to his or her own children.

We all have a fundamental need to belong, to feel safe, alive, and welcome. We can transform our own family or household into such a place where this is possible. Together we can practice breathing and smiling, sitting together, drinking tea together in mindfulness. If we have a bell, the bell is also part of the community, because the bell helps us practice, calling us back to ourselves to the present moment. If we have a meditation cushion, the cushion is also part of the community.

There are many things that help us practice mindfulness—even the air for breathing. If we live near a park or a riverbank, we can enjoy walking meditation there, and the park or river becomes part of our community. We need to establish a community at home. From time to time we can invite a friend to join us. We need to expand our definition of family to include not only our friends and community, but also the sun, the sky, the trees, the birds, and the hills around us. Practicing mindfulness is much easier when we do it together.

Fierce and Gentle Bodhisattva

When you enter the gate of a Buddhist temple, you will probably see the statue of a very gentle figure with a welcoming smile on your left. But on your right, you will see a figure with a very fierce face, brandishing a weapon. His whole face is burning with fury, and smoke and flames are pouring out of his eyes and mouth.

Both of these figures are bodhisattvas—beings who have dedicated their whole life to putting an end to other people's suffering. The fierce figure is the one who has the capacity to keep the hungry ghosts in check. Every time we organize a ceremony to offer food and drink to the hungry ghosts, the lost and wandering souls, we need to evoke the bodhisattva with the burning face to come and help. The hungry ghosts only listen to him because he has the fierce look that says, "You better behave; otherwise you'll get it!" So when you see someone with a fierce face, you can't necessarily say that person is evil. They might be a real bodhisattva. They may look very scary, but deep inside there is the heart of a bodhisattva. You can be very firm, but at the same time you can be very compassionate.

If you are a gentle bodhisattva, you have to have real compassion and understanding within you. If you are the fierce, red-faced bodhisattva and demonstrate firmness and strength, you must also have a tender heart and deep understanding.

The Astronaut

Imagine an astronaut going to the moon. After he lands on the moon, something goes wrong with the spacecraft and he can't blast off again to return to planet Earth. At NASA mission control in Houston, they are unable to contact him. He knows he only has enough oxygen to last a short time, not enough time for people to come and rescue him. In those last moments of his life, what do you think he thinks about? What does he want?

On the moon, it's not possible to walk mindfully like we do on earth. All you can do is jump because there's so little gravity. Perhaps the astronaut remembers how beautiful it is on Earth. When we look up at the moon from the Earth, we may think the moon is so beautiful. But if we're on the moon and looking back at the Earth, we see Earth's magnificence.

We have lived on this planet for so many years, and yet have we truly been in touch with the wonders of life on Earth? We argue with one person, we're jealous of another, we run after this and chase after that, and we become blind to the beauties all around us. We don't realize what a miracle it is to be able to walk on this beautiful planet.

If the astronaut stranded on the moon were asked what he would like most of all, he would probably say that his greatest wish would be to return to Earth. He wouldn't want a new car or a new house. Probably all he would want would be to walk on this beautiful planet Earth. All other desires would pale into insignificance.

Luckily at the last moment, a rescue ship arrives, and the astronaut is able to return to Earth. We are all like that rescued astronaut. We have the capacity to take happy, light, and free steps on our beautiful planet Earth. We need to remember how precious this is.

While practicing mindful walking, we have a chance to enter into deep communion with the planet Earth and realize that Earth is our home. One breath, one step is all we need to feel at home and comfortable in the here and now. With each breath, you can bring your body and your mind back to the present moment. You don't have to run after anything anymore. The Earth is right here; you feel completely satisfied with the present moment. Nothing is missing.

Mindful walking is something that can bring us great happiness. Each of our steps nourishes our heart, our mind, and our body. We have far more conditions for happiness than we realize. Walking meditation is one way of returning to ourselves. We can return within the snap of a finger. It takes a long time to go to the moon and back, but it only takes one breath to return to your true home.

Autumn Leaf

One day as I was about to step on a dry leaf, I stopped. Looking closely, I saw that the leaf was not really dead; it was merging with the moist soil and preparing to appear on the tree the following spring in another form. I smiled at the leaf and said, "You are just pretending."

Everything is pretending to be born and pretending to die, including the leaf I almost stepped on. The Buddha said, "When conditions are sufficient, the body reveals itself, and we say the body *is*. When conditions are not sufficient, the body cannot be perceived by us, and we say the body *is not*." The day of our so-called death is a day of our continuation in many other forms. Touching this truth is a deep practice, and brings us relief from our deepest fears.

Nirvana means extinction, the extinction of all notions and concepts, including the concepts of birth, death, being, nonbeing, coming, and going. Nirvana is the ultimate dimension of life, a state of coolness, peace, and joy. It is not a state to be attained after death. You can touch nirvana right now by breathing, walking, and drinking your tea in mindfulness.

Finding Home

I once heard the story of a young Japanese American man who went into a café. While he was drinking his coffee, he overheard two young men talking in Vietnamese and crying. The Japanese American man asked them why they were crying, and one of the Vietnamese men said, "We can't go back to our homeland. The government there has forbidden us from going back."

Visibly upset, the Japanese American said, "That is no reason to cry. Even though you may be exiled and unable to return, at least you still have a country, a place where you belong. I don't have a country to go back to. I was born and raised in the US and although I look Japanese, culturally I'm American. But Americans don't truly accept me; they see me as an Asian, a foreigner. So I went back to Japan and tried to make it my home. But when I arrived there, the Japanese said I didn't speak or act like a Japanese person, so they didn't accept me either. Even though I have an American passport, even though I can go to Japan, I do not have a home. But you do."

There are many young people who were born and raised in the US, but who do not feel they are accepted as Americans by other Americans. They feel sad and want to go back to find their home. They think: "If my home is not in America, it has to be somewhere else." But they don't fit in with their country of origin either. Very few of us feel we are in our true home. Even if we are lucky enough to have a nationality, a citizenship, and a passport, many of us are still searching for where we belong.

Do you have a home? Do you have a true home where you feel comfortable, peaceful, and free?

There are US citizens who have been living in the country for a long time, often for generations, but still don't feel welcome. In

Vietnam there are many people who don't feel accepted or understood by their country or that they have a future there, and so they want to leave.

Who among us has a true home? Who feels comfortable at home in their own country? I have a home, and I feel very comfortable in my home, even though I have been exiled from Vietnam for almost forty years. Despite my exile, I don't suffer, because I have found my true home. My true home is not in Plum Village in France. My true home is not in the United States. My true home is not limited to a particular place or time.

My true home cannot be defined in terms of place or culture. It's simplistic to say that in terms of culture or nationality I am Vietnamese. I don't have a Vietnamese passport or identity card, so legally speaking, I am not Vietnamese. Genetically there is no such race as the "Vietnamese" race. Looking into me, you can see Melanesian, Indonesian, Mongolian, and African elements. In fact, the Vietnamese race is made entirely of non-Vietnamese elements. That is true for any nationality. Seeing that can set us free. The whole cosmos has come together in order to help you to manifest.

Life Is Our True Home

In the Buddhist tradition, a session of sitting meditation always begins with the sound of the bell. This sound is a gentle reminder to come home to ourselves.

Our true home is the present moment, whatever is happening right here and right now. Our true home is a place without discrimination, a place without hatred. Our true home is the place where we are no longer seeking anything, no longer yearning for anything, no longer regretting anything. When we return to right here and right now with the energy of mindfulness, we will be able to establish our true home in the present moment.

Your true home is something you have to create for yourself. When we know how to make peace with our body, to take care of our body, and release the tension in our body, then our body becomes a comfortable, peaceful home for us to come back to in the present moment. When we know how to take care of our feelings—when we know how to generate joy and happiness, and how to handle a painful feeling—we can cultivate and restore a happy home in the present moment. And when we know how to generate the energies of understanding and compassion, our home will be a very cozy, pleasant place to come back to. But if we're not able to do these things, we won't want to go home. Home is not something to hope for, but to cultivate. There is no way home; home is the way.

Liberation lies in the present moment. We can be in touch with all our spiritual and blood ancestors right in the present moment. We need to learn how to come back to the present moment, and penetrate that moment, in order to discover our true home. When we can feel these ancestors with us in the present moment, we no longer need to worry or suffer. When we stop trying to find our home outside ourselves—in space, time, culture, territory, nationality, or race—we can find true happiness.

Our true home is not an abstract idea. It is a solid reality that we can touch with our feet, our hands, and our mind in every moment. If we know this, then nobody can take away our true home. Even if people occupy our country or put us in prison, we still have our true home, and no one can ever take it away. I speak to those of you who feel that you have never had a home. I speak to the parents who feel that the country they left is no longer their home, but that the new country is not their home yet either. Each one of us can practice to find our true home and to help our children find their true home also.

You may wonder if the most wonderful moments of your life are already behind you. Or you may think the happiest moment of your life is still to come. But this is the moment we have been waiting for. The Buddha said, "You have to make the *present* moment into the most wonderful moment of your life."

I Am Not in Here

I have a disciple in Vietnam who wants to build a stupa for my ashes when I die. He and others want to include a plaque with the words "Here lies my beloved teacher." I told them not to waste the temple land. "Do not put me in a small pot and put me in there!" I said. "I don't want to continue like that. It would be better to scatter the ashes outside to help the trees to grow."

I suggested that, if they still insist on building a stupa, they have the plaque say, "I am not in here." But in case people don't get it, they could add a second plaque, "I am not out there either." If people still don't understand, then you can write on the third and last plaque, "I may be found in your way of breathing and walking."

This body of mine will disintegrate, but my actions will continue me. In my daily life, I always practice to see my continuation all around me. We don't need to wait until the total dissolution of this body to continue—we continue in every moment. If you think that I am only this body, then you have not truly seen me. When you look at my friends, you see my continuation. When you see someone walking with mindfulness and compassion, you know he is my continuation. I don't see why we have to say "I will die," because I can already see myself in you, in other people, and in future generations.

Even when the cloud is not there, it continues as snow or rain. It is impossible for a cloud to die. It can become rain or ice, but it cannot become nothing. The cloud does not need to have a soul in order to continue. There's no beginning and no end. I will never die. There will be a dissolution of this body, but that does not mean my death. I will continue, always.

About Thich Nhat Hanh

Thich Nhat Hanh was born Nguyen Xuan Bao in 1926 in Central Vietnam during the French colonial occupation. In his youth, he was deeply affected by images of the Buddha radiating peace in stark contrast to the strife and suffering he witnessed all around him. At sixteen he asked his parents' permission to become a monk, and he entered Tu Hieu monastery in Hue, ordaining as a novice monk in the Linji (Japanese: Rinzai) school of the Vietnamese Zen tradition.

The fundamental training of a novice in Vietnam is essentially to practice being present in every moment and to do whatever one is doing with full awareness. Nhat Hanh lived amongst the forests and gardens of Tu Hieu with his community of brother monks, studying and practicing under the guidance of the abbot, a wise and experienced teacher who loved and understood his students.

After three years, Nhat Hanh left Tu Hieu to attend the Buddhist Institute in Hue. He then went to Saigon, the center of the movement to renew Buddhism and make it relevant to people's everyday lives and the reality of modern society. He helped to found Van Hanh University, an Institute of Higher Buddhist Studies, and he became the editor of the journal *Vietnamese Buddhism*, which gave creative Buddhist thinkers a voice and encouraged the unification of all the schools of Buddhism in Vietnam.

The journal was closed down after two years by the conservative Buddhist leadership. Nhat Hanh continued to teach and write, and his writings continued to be opposed by the Buddhist leadership and the increasingly repressive and dictatorial Diem regime.

In 1962 Nhat Hanh went to the US to study comparative religion at Princeton University. In 1963 he was offered a teaching position at Columbia University. After the fall of the Diem regime in 1963, the

Buddhist leadership was more open to reform, so Nhat Hanh cut short his stay in the US and returned to Vietnam in 1964 to see the fulfillment of a dream, the founding of the Unified Buddhist Church, which brought together all the various Buddhist congregations of Vietnam.

The war in Vietnam continued to escalate, causing more and more chaos and devastation in the towns and countryside. Whole villages were destroyed, resulting in many refugees. In 1964 Nhat Hanh founded the School of Youth for Social Service (SYSS), training young social workers, both monastic and lay, to go into villages, live amongst the people, help them rebuild and reorganize their villages, and help refugees relocate. Because Nhat Hanh and the SYSS workers refused to take any side other than the side of helping people, they were viewed with suspicion by the Communist and pro-American forces alike. But their love, dedication, and ethical way of working won the hearts of many people. Many of Nhat Hanh's students, friends, and colleagues were killed or injured during this time.

As the war continued to intensify, Nhat Hanh decided to return to the source of the war, traveling to Washington to call for peace and going on a North American speaking tour to inform people in the United States of the devastating effects of the war on the people of Vietnam. It was at this time that Nhat Hanh met and made a deep impression on the Trappist monk Thomas Merton, Secretary of Defense Robert McNamara, and Dr. Martin Luther King Jr., who later nominated him for the Nobel Peace Prize. When the government of South Vietnam heard of these activities, they refused to let Nhat Hanh return to Vietnam, and he became an exile in the West, eventually settling in France.

This was a lonely and difficult time for Nhat Hanh. There were very few Vietnamese people outside Vietnam at the time. Everything he knew, his work, and his students were back in Vietnam. But gradually he came to know the people, trees, birds, and the fruits and flowers of the West. He made friends with adults and children in whatever country he found himself, and he began to feel at home everywhere. Wherever he went, he befriended people, whether they were Catholic priests, Protestant ministers, rabbis, imams, or trade or humanitarian workers. Nhat Hanh continued to go on speaking tours in North America, Europe, and Asia, sharing his methods of practice and voicing the desire of the Vietnamese people for peace. In 1969 he became the representative of the Buddhist Peace Delegation at the Paris Peace Accords, and was able to express the desire of the Vietnamese people for an end to the war.

The end of the war came finally in 1975, but the Communist regime, the new government of Vietnam, was also not willing to allow Nhat Hanh to return home. The Unified Buddhist Church was outlawed, and many of its leading monks were imprisoned. In 1976, while at a conference in Singapore, he heard of the plight of the Vietnamese boatpeople, refugees from Vietnam who had left their country by boat. Many of them died at sea. In unseaworthy boats with little or no food and water, they were at the mercy of storms and sea pirates. If they finally reached shore, they were often pushed back out to sea because many countries would not accept boat-people or had very low quotas for accepting refugees.

Nhat Hanh and his colleagues rented boats, and joined by friends from Europe, brought food and water to the boatpeople, trying to make arrangements with everyone from fishermen and police to government officials, in order to find a place for the boatpeople to land. At the same time they were making efforts to inform the world of the plight of these refugees in an attempt to influence governments around the world to increase their quotas and allow the boatpeople to resettle.

Upon his return from Singapore, Nhat Hanh continued to live in France and to lead retreats and share his teachings in many countries. He continued to support social work efforts in Vietnam and to work for the release of imprisoned monks. He founded a hermitage, the Sweet Potato Community, outside Paris where he went to walk in the forest, grow vegetables, write, and practice.

When this became too small for the number of students who wanted to come and practice with him, Nhat Hanh founded Plum Village in 1982, a practice center and monastery in southwest France, where he still lives. There are currently nine practice centers and monasteries worldwide, in the US, Europe, Asia, and Australia, where his monastic students, today numbering over six hundred, share mindfulness practices in what is now known as the Plum Village Tradition. There are also over one thousand lay Sanghas, communities of people practicing together, worldwide.

In 2004 the Vietnamese government invited Nhat Hanh to visit Vietnam after almost forty years of exile. During his three-month visit in 2005, he led retreats for monks, nuns, and laypeople—mostly young people from all over the world. He had in-depth exchanges with leaders of the Buddhist community as well as with leaders of the government and Communist Party. He returned again in 2007, this time to lead ceremonies to commemorate those who had died in the war and to bring peace, healing, and reconciliation to the survivors, so their suffering would not be passed on to the younger generations. He visited Vietnam for the last time in 2008.

Nhat Hanh continued to travel relentlessly throughout the world to teach and lead retreats, right up until late 2014, when he suffered a serious stroke. In an extraordinary teaching career spanning sixty-five years, Nhat Hanh has taught hundreds of thousands of people, on every continent and from every walk of life. He has led retreats for families, health-care workers, business people, veterans, young people, psychotherapists, teachers, artists, environmentalists, members of congress, and parliamentarians. Many of these students and friends refer to Nhat Hanh affectionately as "Thay," which means "teacher" in Vietnamese. On his eightieth birthday, when asked if he planned to retire, Nhat Hanh said, "Teaching is not done by talking alone. It is done by how you live your life. My life is my teaching. My life is my message."

Related Titles by Thich Nhat Hanh

Answers from the Heart

Being Peace

Cultivating the Mind of Love

The Energy of Prayer

Healing, Sister Dang Nghiem

The Hermit and the Well

Hermitage Among the Clouds

Love Letter to the Earth

The Mindfulness Survival Kit

My Master's Robe

No Mud No Lotus

The Other Shore

Present Moment, Wonderful Moment

**PARALLAX
PRESS**

Parallax Press, a nonprofit publisher founded by Zen Master Thich Nhat Hanh, publishes books and media on the art of mindful living and Engaged Buddhism. We are committed to offering teachings that help transform suffering and injustice. Our aspiration is to contribute to collective insight and awakening, bringing about a more joyful, healthy, and compassionate society.

Monastics and visitors practice the art of mindful living in the tradition of Thich Nhat Hanh at our mindfulness practice centers around the world. To reach any of these communities, or for information about how individuals, couples, and families can join in a retreat, please contact:

Plum Village
33580 Dieulivol, France
plumvillage.org

Asian Institute of Applied Buddhism
Lantau Island, Hong Kong
pvfhk.org

Magnolia Grove Monastery
Batesville, MS 38606, USA
magnoliagrovemonastery.org

La Maison de l'Inspir
93160 Noisy le Grand, France
maisondelinspir.org

Blue Cliff Monastery
Pine Bush, NY 12566, USA
bluecliffmonastery.org

Healing Spring Monastery
77510 Verdelot, France
healingspringmonastery.org

Deer Park Monastery
Escondido, CA 92026, USA
deerparkmonastery.org

Stream Entering Monastery
Beaufort, Victoria 3373, Australia
nhapluu.org

European Institute of
Applied Buddhism
D-51545 Waldbröl, Germany
eiab.eu

Thailand Plum Village
Nakhon Ratchasima
30130 Thailand
thaiplumvillage.org

The Mindfulness Bell, a journal of the art of mindful living in the tradition of Thich Nhat Hanh, is published three times a year by our community. To subscribe or to see the worldwide directory of Sanghas, or local mindfulness groups, visit mindfulnessbell.org.

The Thich Nhat Hanh Foundation supports Thich Nhat Hanh's peace work and mindfulness teachings around the world. For more information on how you can help or on how to nourish your mindfulness practice, visit the foundation at tnhf.org.